FULL-FRONTAL NERDITY

Lessons in Loving and Living with Your Brain

K.S. WISWELL

This publication is designed to provide accurate information in regard to the subject matter covered as of its publication date, with the understanding that knowledge and best practice constantly evolve. The publisher is not engaged in rendering medical, legal, accounting, or other professional service. If medical or legal advice or other expert assistance is required, the services of a competent professional should be sought. This publication is not intended for use in clinical practice or the delivery of medical care. To the fullest extent of the law, neither the Publisher nor the Editors assume any liability for any injury and/or damage to persons or property arising out of or related to any use of the material contained in this book.

Published by 750 Publishing
750 Third Avenue
New York, NY 10017

10 9 8 7 6 5 4 3 2 1

ISBN: 978-1-5062-4987-2

For all the teachers.

(Especially the two who raised me.)

FULL-FRONTAL NERDITY: PROSPECTUS

From the age of zero, I was the tortured rope in a tug-of-war between my left brain and my right. Albert Einstein or Katharine Hepburn? Math team or music? Scientist or storyteller? I could never choose. And so, with the wisdom of Solomon on Opposite Day, I glued the baby back together and simply nerded out in every direction.

Being a Nerd-of-All-Trades has been rewarding, exhilarating, and often eye-opening, but it has also brought its challenges. It can be difficult viewing life with the analytical eye of an academic when everyone around you is guided foremost by emotion, and it can be even harder dealing with emotions that make little sense to your logical brain. As soon as the cocoon of academia burst open, I had to learn how to be a functioning human in the real world, and out here not as many people laugh at your historically-accurate limericks about the High King of Ireland.

My wandering path from student at Harvard to writer in Hollywood led me through the corporate maze and the freelance jungle, included management and grunt work, and bestowed both financial abundance and starving artistry. To paraphrase Joni Mitchell, I've looked at life from most sides, now – and while it hasn't always been pretty, it has often been hilarious.

Full-Frontal Nerdity is a collection of some of the stories, thought experiments, and epiphanies I've lived along the way, offered both for schadenfreude and the chance to learn the lessons of my experience without having to make the mistakes yourself. Taking inspiration from the many subjects that have sparked my curiosity over the years – statistics, mythology, physics, poetry, and even the history of pi – this book aims to give insight into the everyday mysteries and struggles of being a thinking person in an often-irrational world.

I hope to introduce you to some fascinating concepts, maybe even revisit some you already know, and explore the more practical lessons to be gleaned from applying those subjects to daily life. Instead of keeping it in the classroom, these essays – both rigorous and comical – encourage fully embracing your nerdity to achieve newfound depths of understanding about living, loving, and simply *being* in our humorously alien universe.

Smart is sexy, but people can make it really difficult to believe that sometimes. Let me show you the hard-earned solace that comes from learning to love – and live with – your brain.

FULL-FRONTAL NERDITY: SYLLABUS

102: RELATIONSHIPS

103: LIFE (STRIVING)

104: LIFE (COPING)

EXTRA CREDIT

FULL-FRONTAL NERDITY: COMMENCEMENT

WHERE WE BEGIN

POMPOUS AND CIRCUMSTANTIAL

Not too long ago, Natalie Portman and I both returned to our mutual alma mater to perform at commencement. One of us wore her old band jacket and played a French horn in order to gain free admission, and the other had been invited by the university to deliver the commencement address, but I'll let you guess which was which. In all seriousness, it was refreshing to hear Natalie recount the experience of first setting foot in such an overwhelming and impressive place full of overwhelming and impressive people – and comforting to learn that despite being impressive herself when she arrived, she made many of the same mistakes I did.

The world is full of brazenly confident people, and Harvard Yard has more than its fair share. Natalie remembered five different peers who announced on Day One that they would be President someday; I only remember hearing it from two people on my first day, but both Natalie and I believed all of them based on the sheer force of their conviction. Bold declarations are impressive, and those of us not in the habit of making our own are inclined to be won over by their swagger.

(This is the only explanation for a particularly disastrous dating choice of mine freshman year; he told me he was the smartest, funniest guy in the room and I believed him. He was wrong.)

As I quickly learned, often through pain and shame, there is no guarantee of any substance behind the bluster, and it is worth your while to consider the source. For every Babe Ruth who backs up a called shot there are a dozen Donald Trumps who are full of empty sound and fury.

Both Natalie and I reacted to our bold new world in the same way: by letting it intimidate us. We accepted these people's brazen visions of the world, their standards for greatness, and their definitions of success. Instead of asking ourselves what *we* wanted out of school or life, we worried about not being good enough to live up to their expectations – and once someone else is allowed to make up the rules, there really is no way to come out on top. Just try to play a game with any six-year-old.

Whenever I find myself falling back into that wide-eyed freshman mindset, I think about Albert Einstein and remember his "Annus Mirabilis" – the one year (1905) in which he published four papers, each a major breakthrough in its own right. Talk about someone able to back up his swagger.

One of the recurring themes in discussions of Einstein's unparalleled achievement is the complete unwillingness he had to ever accept any unproven principle as a given. No assumptions – prove it or lose it. And because Albert Einstein refused to believe time was an immutable constant simply because everyone else assumed it was and no one had seen evidence to the contrary, he was free to explore his own imaginings, and now the world understands relativity. You're welcome, world.

When we free ourselves from belief in how things are "supposed to" be, we open the door to far deeper understanding and far greater achievement. If we remain oblivious to the limitations assumed by the world, those limits may no longer apply. As Natalie put it in her speech, "my complete ignorance to my own limitations…got me into the director's chair."

Or, to say it as that six-year-old would put it: "Oh yeah? Sez who?"

Look to the bumblebee for inspiration. For centuries, the world of physics expended a great deal of energy and vapors over the fact that a short, fat, fuzzy insect with stubby wings should not be able to fly. And yet they fly anyway. Mainly, as mathematician Sir Michael Atiyah pointed out, because a bumblebee does not understand the laws of thermodynamics. It simply doesn't know it can't fly.*

If *Forrest Gump* taught us anything, it is that if we dive into that box of chocolates listening to cries of "beware the cherry cordial" and "butter creams are the best" we will very likely get in our own way and wind up disappointed, but if we go in hoping for a sweet treat, we will probably get one. At least I think that was the point.

---

*Also, as science finally determined, because it doesn't flap its wings up and down like other flying things but rather front-to-back with a slight tilt, as though treading water, which creates mini hurricanes above each wing, with low-pressure centers that make it easier to stay aloft. But "because of ignorance" is more romantic.

To quote Stephen Colbert's 2015 commencement address at Wake Forest, "having your own standards allows you to perceive success where others may see failure." So in other words, don't believe everything people say (especially about themselves), don't believe everything you think (especially about yourself), and define your own standards for success and happiness. Then work for them. Everyone else can go suck a cherry cordial.

Full-Frontal Nerdity 101: Love

LESSON 1
ASTROPHYSICS

THE SEARCH FOR SIGNS OF INTELLIGENT LIFE PARTNERS IN THE UNIVERSE

Confession time: I write romantic comedies, and I do not believe in The One.

Before anyone takes away my pen and paper, let me clarify – this is not a Nicholas Sparks situation where my cynical outlook toward humanity and borderline-misogynist opinion of women drives me to churn out one crassly formulaic story after another. I absolutely believe in love, soul mates, true partners, and all that crap; I just don't believe each of us has only One.

Both my head and my heart reject the idea. Already, in my short time on Earth experimenting with love, I have met at least two men with whom I am sure I could have enjoyed spending the rest of my life. The fact that things didn't work out doesn't make them – or our relationships – any less wonderful.

As for my brain, the idea of The One is straight-up depressing on a practical level. There are 7.2 billion people on the planet, most of whom – even *with* the internet – we will never meet. What if someone's One lives in North Korea? Tough noogies?

But I prefer proof and reason when possible, and in this particular situation astrophysics can provide: The Drake Equation is a formula developed in 1961 by astronomer Frank Drake to calculate the probability we will ever detect intelligent alien life in the universe. Since men are from Mars and women Venereal, I figure it is equally applicable to determining the odds of our search for soul mates in the human universe.

While the actual Drake Equation is impossible to calculate (so far) because most of its variables are unknown (for now), it is still pretty simple in essence and easy to apply to an area that is better known (like people). The original equation is just a straight multiplication of the probabilities of various factors necessary for finding E.T. – like that aliens exist in the first place, or have detectable technology.

Specifically, (hang in there) it looks like this:

$$N = R \times Fp \times Ne \times Fl \times Fi \times Fc \times L$$

which looks completely like gibberish until you know what all the shorthand stands for. And once you know that, you can apply it to human dating. Let's do it!

N stands for the number of alien civilizations we can detect. In other words, it is the answer we are looking for – it is the number of The Ones.

R is the rate at which stars form in the universe, so for mate searching it is the rate at which humans form (unless you're into something else – no judgment). According to P.T. Barnum, there's a sucker born every minute, so let's say R = 1/min.

Fp is the fraction of stars in the universe hosting planets. Equivalently, let's call it the fraction of persons with the proper criteria for one's sexual orientation. For most that will be at minimum half the population, possibly more depending on how far along the Kinsey scale you stretch toward pansexual, but then minus the members of your preferred gender that do not prefer *your* gender*. In short, this number will be different for everyone, but as I am a heterosexual woman, let's go with 40% for this exercise. (Gallup estimates just over 5% of the population identifies as LGBT, but that is up to 8% with younger generations, plus people have secrets, so I bumped it up to 10%.) Okay, that means in our formula Fp = 2/5.

Ne is the fraction of planets that pass the "Goldilocks" test, or in other words are suitable to sustain life. For sustaining a this-could-become-forever relationship, this would be the fraction of the population between, say, 25 and 60, which is about half of humanity. Ne = 1/2

Check in: So far we have $N(\textit{The Ones}) = \dfrac{1}{min} \times \dfrac{2}{5} \times \dfrac{1}{2} \times Fl \times Fi \times Fc \times L$

Fl is the fraction of Goldilocks planets with *actual* life, which in astrophysics is sadly unknown, and which for our purposes I will translate as the fraction who possess viable romantic life.

---

*Hashtag it's complicated.

To define that, we have to take a brief sidebar:

Lists are great for shopping and enemies, but when it comes to relationships they are obstructionist defense mechanisms. I've been with men who were great on paper and terrible in practice, and with men I never would have picked out of a lineup who made me blissfully happy. Superficial trappings are meaningless, but no relationship can survive without "PIE" – a triumvirate of elements that are the only food that matters. The three slices of PIE are Physical attraction, Intellectual stimulation, and Emotional support. A relationship with all three will always be viable, while the absence of any will leave you hungry forever.

So, if we're looking for the fraction of partners who possess viable romantic life, we're looking for the ones with the first piece of PIE: Physical attraction. This is where things get harder to calculate. Let's say I've met about 25,000 people so far in my lifetime. (Various minds have entertained the question of how many people one meets over a lifetime, and estimates vary from as low as 10,000 to somewhere around 80-100,000 for more urban dwellers. I have lived in three major cities, traveled a lot, and been a performer all my life, but I'm also an introvert and only a third of the way through my life. So, 25,000 is fair.) In a room full of, say, 25 random people aged 25-60, I'm probably going to be physically attracted to one (not everywhere is Los Angeles), and let's be neutral in our self-esteem and say there is a 50% chance that person will feel a mutual spark. Which out of the 25,000 in my life means there have been about 500 people with whom I have shared enough attraction to have sex (don't worry, Dad, I didn't). So that makes Fl = 500/25,000, or 1/50.

Fi is the fraction of life-bearing planets with *intelligent* life, and that perfectly corresponds to the second piece of PIE: Intellectual stimulation. I'd say I've met at least 50 sexy, heterosexual men I felt I could keep talking to forever, and 50 out of 500 is 1/10. Fi = 1/10

Fc is the fraction of intelligent life that possesses the technology to make themselves detectable. For a life partner, that means having the last piece of the PIE: Emotional maturity, or the ability to sustain an actual committed relationship. There have really only been two men (so far) in my experience with all three pieces of PIE, so this last fraction is 2/50, or Fc = 1/25.

Check in: now we have $N(\text{The Ones}) = \dfrac{1}{min} \times \dfrac{2}{5} \times \dfrac{1}{2} \times \dfrac{1}{50} \times \dfrac{1}{10} \times \dfrac{1}{25} \times L$

Lastly comes **L**, which in the Drake Equation represents the length of time any technologically advanced alien race will remain actually detectable. For our civilization, it has only been about 100 years so far – since we started broadcasting into the atmosphere. In terms of romance with humans, this is the Serious Dating Window – when a person is ready, able, and looking, but not yet nailed down. Let's allow for life to get in the way and set that window at about 15 years. With

365.25 days per year, 24 hours per day, and 60 minutes per hour, there are in fact 525,960 minutes per year* which comes to L = 7,889,400 minutes.

Putting it all together, we can see that *my* N (number of 'Ones') equals: 1 sucker per minute, times 2/5 who are heterosexual men, times 1/2 at a datable age, times 1/50 who are physically attracting, times 1/10 also intellectually stimulating, times 1/25 with the trifecta of emotional maturity, all multiplied by 7,889,400 minutes of partner seeking.

$$N(\textit{The Ones}) = \frac{1}{min} \times \frac{2}{5} \times \frac{1}{2} \times \frac{1}{50} \times \frac{1}{10} \times \frac{1}{25} \times 7,889,400 min$$

The result: 126 and a quarter. Rounding up, there are 127 The Ones for me on Earth.

Of course, my numbers are largely anecdotal and would never pass the scrutiny of peer review, but the point remains – no way is there only One perfect partner. In fact, if we use the *actual* rate of human birth instead of P.T. Barnum's – 258 per minute – my number comes out to be **32,567 The Ones**. Which is almost exactly the population of Bray, Ireland. (Bring on the gingers!)

32,600 ideal potential mates seems like a lot (32,600 redheaded potential mates sounds like heaven), but that's *on the whole planet*. Add in that we also have to meet, and (preferably) speak the same language, and both be available at the same time... the number whittles down quickly. If we're lucky, we experience maybe a handful in our lifetime. *And then they have to want the relationship too.*

---

*Rent lied to us!

When you consider that a "forever" relationship requires three major things to happen in unison – first, we have to be ready for the responsibility ourselves; second, we have to meet one of the 32,567 potential partners; and third, that person has to also want us – it is no wonder it feels like there is only One magical person out there. But it still only *feels* that way.

Despair is silly, but patience is definitely called for. Or, perhaps, a move to Bray, Ireland.

LESSON 2
LINGUISTICS
WILL YOU BE MY EGGPLANT?

In college, there was this boy. He had red hair, so I of course liked him immediately, but he was also sweet and goofy, had a beautiful singing voice, and played the French horn, like me, which is how we met. Over the years, we never quite managed to get it together, but there was a lot of "almost." I liked him, but he didn't know it; then he liked me, but I had met my first love; I was single again, but by then he had a girlfriend… you know the drill. Our hearts were two magnets with misaligned polarity – naturally attracted to each other, but destined to repel one another every time we got too close. Maybe if one of us had just flipped the other over we could have made the connection, but we were teenagers; what did we know?

Even though we never managed to find our way into couple-dom, our mutual attraction and tumultuous relationship was apparent to everyone around us. Plus, we were band geeks, which is like being under surveillance by your incestuous family while starring in a reality TV show. Everyone is up in everyone's business, is what I'm saying. We got a *lot* of questions along the way. "Are you two dating?" "Do you like him?" "Is he your boyfriend?" "Is this a thing or something?" "What *are* you guys?"

When you're nineteen, you may know in your gut that the appropriate answer to all of these questions is, "None of your damn business," but the nerve to actually say that is still a long way off. Still, I didn't have much inclination to get into a personal conversation about a relationship I could barely quantify myself, and even if I had wanted to, there was no easy way to answer. I didn't *know* what we were; it was complicated. So one day, in response to the latest nosy inquiry about the real deal with this boy, I simply answered, "He's my eggplant."

I have no idea why that particular word popped into my head at that moment. It certainly wasn't because of what the eggplant implies *now*, since emojis weren't yet even a twinkle in the internet's eye. (Is it possible I made that happen? Should I ask for royalties?) Perhaps it was because I have always considered the eggplant to be a ridiculously named object. How did that even happen? "Plant" I can understand, but they are not the size or shape of eggs, or egg colored* or the texture of eggs, and certainly not egg flavored. "Eggplant" is the exact opposite of an onomatopoeia – it is a thing that does not look, sound, or in any way resemble the word used to describe it. We should have a name for that. It's an "Offomatopoeia."

We should have a word for a lot of things that don't have names, which was kind of my point by calling this boy my eggplant (in addition to the point that the people doing the nosing should butt out). For all of the nuance of the English

---

*There *are* small white eggplants, and that's how it got its name in English. I learned that later, as an adult who eats vegetables.

language – and I do love this language – the pickings are pretty slim when it comes to the stages of romance. Fights will break out over the subtle differences between "geeks", "dorks", and "nerds", but when it comes to love, the best distinction our language can muster is "love," "platonic love," and "*in* love." No wonder poor Kevin Arnold had to ask if Winnie Cooper just "liked" him, or if she "*like* liked" him.

In relationships, our descriptors are pathetic. Once there is a level of commitment, it is pretty easy: spouse, partner, fiancé, boyfriend, girlfriend, significant other. But there are a whole lot of relationship stages before two people get to that point, and for those our language simply has no label. What are we supposed to call someone we *like* like, or are just starting to date, or are just starting to *seriously* date? (Even in describing the relationship phases our vocabulary is pretty limited.) We could call him a "prospect," but this isn't the NFL draft. A "candidate"? That's way too political. She could be a "contender," but that's way too Brando. How about a "person of interest?" Sure, if you want it to sound like you're investigating her for murder. And what about someone we're just sleeping with? (Or: nailing, screwing, banging, tapping, shagging, humping – here the vocabulary is practically endless.) There is the term "lover," but I think Will Ferrell and Rachel Dratch pretty much killed that one forever.

We'd probably be better off if we didn't label things at all, but since we do, there should at least be enough labels to go around. Instead, there is a linguistic shaming of people outside of committed relationships (the single, unwed, available, unattached…), and I for one am not okay with it. Calling the romantic protagonists in my life "eggplant" – which I continue to do – is my one-woman protest (objection, disruption, act of defiance, stand…). What do you say we see if it can catch on? Maybe we can start an uprising (revolution, rebellion, movement, coup…). Or maybe we'll just get some people to mind their own business. Either way works for me.

LESSON 3
PROBABILITY
LOVE, DAMNED LOVE, AND STATISTICS

Okay, geek squad, let's get down and nerdy for a little bit. Fair warning: the math in today's session will be a little more rigorous than the Drake Equation. I promise to make it fun (says the former captain of her high school math team), and I assure you there will be no test after. To every student past, present, and future who ever rolled their eyes to the heavens in math class and asked, "When am I *ever* going to use this in real life?" I answer with the eternal wisdom of Shania Twain: "From this moment on."

The subject at hand is Bayesian reasoning, which is a school of probabilistic thinking employed by, among others, the most successful gamblers. Anyone who has ever used OK Cupid or eaten at a Taco Bell can tell you that life is a gamble, so I naturally wondered how Bayesian reasoning might apply to areas more relevant to me than sports betting. Like, say, conducting myself in affairs of the heart. Now, I consider myself a fairly logical and scientific individual – mostly because I am ridiculously logical and scientific – but what Bayesian reasoning made me realize about my approach to human interaction kind of blew my mind. Mister Spock I was *not*.

A little background: Thomas Bayes was an 18th century English minister who sought to resolve the paradox of a benevolent God and the existence of evil. See? I told you this would be fun. In very brief terms (my apologies to any theologians or philosophers our there), his answer revolved around the idea that the imperfections we see in the world are ours, not God's, because our knowledge is never complete. In other words, if we see too much evil in the world, it doesn't mean that there isn't overall good, but rather that we are not seeing the whole picture. I'll save the larger debate about good versus evil for my next *Lord of the Rings* party, but what matters most is that Bayes introduced the concept that humans learn about the world through approximation rather than certainty – getting closer and closer to the truth with each new piece of the puzzle, but never knowing the absolute truth. *And being okay with that.*

Bayes's chief rival in those days was David Hume, a Scottish philosopher to whom I'm going to give the benefit of the doubt and assume was drunk a lot, because he equated rational belief with certainty. Talk about depressing. Here's a quick example to demonstrate the disparity: imagine you have moved to Los Angeles with no prior knowledge of its climate, history, or reputation, presumably because you have never seen a movie, read a book, watched TV, or met a Californian. This makes you either an alien or Amish, but I digress. Day 1: it is sunny. Aw, that's nice. Day 2: sunny again. Cool. Perhaps this is a trend. Day 3: still more sun, and so on, and so on. The Bayesian thinker will grow more confident with each passing day that tomorrow's weather is likely to be sunny – never fully reaching

100% certainty, mind you, but getting darn close. Even when, 300 days in, it suddenly rains (yes, we experience epic droughts here in LA), the Bayesian will still be pretty sure the next day will be sunny, because the balance of the available evidence is 300 days of sun to one of rain. Those on Team Hume, on the other hand, reason that since we can't be certain about tomorrow's weather, it is equally rational to predict sun and rain. This sounds like a pretty high-stress way of life to me, and a recipe for an early ulcer. No wonder he drank.

Now we're all caught up: Bayesian reasoning balances prior knowledge (what we've learned up to now) with new information to make a probabilistic prediction about what is true and thus avoid overreaction to immediate information, while those on Team Hume remain susceptible to the false positive – when the newest information is given disproportionate importance. I don't know about you, but one seems like a far more productive way to interact with the world. (And if you think it's the second way, well, you should become a Republican Congressperson or work in cable news; you would do well there.)

But when it comes to pursuing the opposite sex, or the same sex, or sex in general, we tend to drop Bayes like a hot potato and make out with Hume every time.

First date went well? We're in love! No word for the next two days? He hates me! Got asked out in a clear, direct way? Hooray, a grown up! Got cancelled on a few days later? What a flake; it's over. In relationships, we tend to ignore the past entirely in favor of how we are feeling *right now* (it's raining today and thus will never be sunny again), *or* deny the probable with the excuse that we can't know for certain (sure, he hasn't called for three weeks, but maybe he was unexpectedly sent to space; YOU don't know). Either way, there is going to be a lot of anxiety and crying over what is – to be all cold and scientific for a second – just one new piece of data.

To be Bayesian in love, we must consider not just the newest information, but also the weight of everything else we have learned up to this point. This is easier said than done, so brace yourself: I'm going to show you how with math.

In Bayes's theorem, when new information comes in (i.e. an event occurs), we must consider three specific things before we can make a probabilistic guess at the truth. Let's make our new event one to which we can all relate: someone asked for your number (email, Twitter handle, Insta, whatever), and then didn't call (text, tweet, DM, you get the idea). According to an entire book and movie franchise, this means without question that they are Just Not That Into You. But to really judge the truth of that feeling, Bayes asks us to evaluate the following:

First is the probability that, if it IS true – they are indeed NOT into you – they would do what they just did: ask for your info and then not connect. This is variable Y. It seems weird that someone *not* into you would ask for your info, so our instinct might initially be to set this probability low. Mine certainly would be, but I am from New England and have learned the hard way that I too frequently assume people are honest. In reality, there is social convention to consider (they just want to be nice), as well as alcohol, the existence of sadists, and the fact that you may be in Los Angeles where people are always hedging their bets. Plus, there is the actual fact of them not calling… so let's say there is a 75% chance of someone NOT that into you asking for your info, but then not calling. Y = 0.75

Next we have to consider the opposite – the probability of someone who IS into you asking for your number but then not connecting. This is variable Z. As a woman, and a creative one at that, I can come up with a million possible reasons for the lack of call: maybe he lost my info, or lost his phone, or maybe he's scared, or hasn't broken up with his current girlfriend yet, or maybe he works for the CIA… But I am going to let the rational part of my brain step in and acknowledge that, while possible, all together there is still at best probably a 20% chance of any of these being true. (Some might say, "Maybe he's busy with work! That happens," to which I speak from experience and reply, unless that work is cave diving or actually going to space, he could find a way to get in touch if he wanted to.) Z = 0.2

Finally, and most importantly, we must consider what Bayesians refer to as the *prior* – the probability *before* the event that the conclusion being judged is true. In this situation, our prior is the probability - before knowing anything about this particular person or event - that *any* person you meet would NOT be into you. This is variable X. This is also where self-esteem comes into play, so let's start with a neutral 50%; some people like me, some don't. Meh. X = 0.5

Once you have assigned those probabilities, the math is pretty simple. The probability of it being true that this new person who did not call or text is, in fact, NOT that into you is the fraction:

$$\frac{XY}{(XY) + Z(1 - X)}$$

In plain English, it is the prior (X) – the probability that a person is not into you – multiplied by the probability they are not into you given this event happened (Y), divided by that same product (XY) *plus* the probability that the prior is *wrong* (1–X) multiplied by the probability of it being wrong – they *are* into you – given this event (Z). With our numbers, that is:

$$\frac{(.5)(.75)}{(.5)(.75) + (.2)(.5)}$$

which comes out to 0.79. So, yeah, there is an almost 80% chance they aren't that into you – but a far cry from the 100% certainty it feels like in the moment and is implied by a kitschy catch phrase. (And the more likely you are to believe a person who is into you would fail to connect – meaning the higher you set Z – the lower the percentage drops.)

What I love most about this demonstration, though, is how it shows with math the effect that our own personal outlook changes the way we react to things (or should react to them, if we're being Bayesian). True, naivete can perpetuate itself, as the higher we set Z, the lower the final probability becomes that a lack of connection indicates disinterest, but Z isn't the only variable that can change. A person with very high self-esteem would probably have a low prior – say, a 10% chance that any random person would NOT be into her. When X gets changed from 0.5 to 0.1 (and Y and Z remain the same), the lack of phone call results in only a 29.5% chance that the non-caller isn't that into you. We become more willing to consider the event a false positive, because it is outweighed by our established understanding of our general likability. But if we have a low opinion of ourselves – say, a prior of 90%* – one missing phone call results in a 97% certainty they aren't into you. Devastating. So, if you find yourself reeling from every little dating hiccup, take a hard look in the mirror and re-evaluate your priors. Also, find a friend to tell you how awesome you are – and *listen*.

Besides protecting us from the imbalanced impact of a false positive, Bayesian reasoning also defends against being that sucker who believes Adam Sandler could actually be a secret agent, because the idea is that we re-assess our reality with each event. Instead of treating *each time* a particular person doesn't call as a new event to be considered independently and given the benefit of the doubt in isolation, we absorb them in sequence and allow them to affect our prior.

One last time, let's set our variables: we will keep Y at 75% and Z and 20%, but let's go for a normal, healthy prior of 30% – there is a 30% chance any random person wouldn't be into you,

---

*and if this is you, listen to some Katy Perry or go hug a Muppet or something, stat.

because you're lovely but some people are dumb. When someone doesn't call the first time, this calculates out to a 61.6% chance they aren't that into you:

$$\frac{(.3)(.75)}{(.3)(.75)+(.2)(.7)} = .616$$

This then becomes our *new prior* for that specific person (rounding down to 60% for the sake of headaches). Now, when we go out and run into this person *again,* and they are flirty and attentive *again,* and then they don't call or communicate *again* (you know who you are), we calculate the probability that this person isn't into us with an X-factor (not to be confused with an American Idol) of 60%:

$$\frac{(.6)(.75)}{(.6)(.75)+(.2)(.4)} = .85$$

That results in an 85% percent likelihood of disinterest. And if it happens a third time (again, you know who you are, and I am *not* amused), the prior starts at 85% and Bayes's theorem calculates a 95.5% chance they are not that into you. Time to write the boy off, for sure!

Bayesian reasoning allows us to avoid overreaction to individual events and also learn and grow from experience, rather than repeat the same mistakes by coming at the world from a place of willful ignorance. Which is exactly what dating *should* be about. Every attempt and false start has something to teach us about what we do or don't want in a relationship, until ideally we know enough to get one right. That is exactly the idea behind Bayes's probabilistic thinking – it is the path, through logic, to less and less wrongness. We can't ever be 100% certain about what is in another person's heart or mind. But if we are willing to apply a little patience and, yes, *math*, we can get to a level of confidence that allows us to trust the right gamble and win big.

ANIMAL HUSBANDRY

I KNOW WHY THE CAGED BIRD CREEPS ME OUT

To be completely judgmental for a moment, you can tell a lot about a potential partner by the type of pet they choose to adopt. (I am ignoring people who have no pets, because these people either have severe allergies or no affection for their fellow living creatures, and clearly those two things are equally awful. The one exception might be those who want a pet but can't have one in their current living situation, but these folks don't have their shit together yet, so let them ripen a bit before dating them.)

Let's start with the usual factions of dog owners and cat owners. Dogs get credit for being devoted while cats are widely considered to be indifferent, but really both species are loyal in their own way. There isn't any more difference between them in that sense than there is between our two political parties, where dogs are Republican ("I will love you forever regardless of logic because you are here and you are giving me attention.") and cats are Democrats ("I will love you forever because you have given me what I want, and I will periodically pretend to not

love you for the sake of my dignity, but who are we kidding?").
Don't ask me about Independents; they're genetic middlers like
hyenas and jackasses.

The real difference between dogs and cats is in the type of energy you choose to invite into your life. Dog owners like drama,
choosing a companion that is shamelessly affectionate, emotionally dependent, and entirely focused on their owner. This is
why dogs are the preferred pet of only children – they provide
elusive companionship along with the feeling of still being the
center of the universe. Dogs basically have borderline personality disorder ("I love you! I love you! Where did you go? When
are you coming back? Why aren't you answering my texts? Are
you dead? Am I dead? Oh, you're home. I love you!"), while
cats live somewhere along the autism spectrum ("You can see
that I love you because I used the litter box instead of your
closet. What more proof do you need?"). Dog owners clearly
opt for high-maintenance relationships, while cat owners are
people who deeply relate to Gwen Stefani singing, "You really
love me underneath it all."

Then there are fish people – straight up narcissists. Owning a
fish is all about selfish pleasure. Almost nothing is required to
keep the fish alive, just clean water and a few food pellets a day.
With a self-cleaning tank, that's literally five seconds of thought.
Meanwhile, the fish provide ambiance, relaxation, beauty, en-
tertainment, escape... the very definition of a one-way relationship. This is why so many children own fish. Is there anything
more narcissistic than a child? Their brains are physically wired
to think only about themselves.

Lizard and snake people are clearly non-conformists, which at least makes them interesting. (I have dated some lovely lizard owners.) They also demonstrate an obvious capacity to see beyond traditional representations of beauty, which is nice. Of course, they *have* chosen a pet that essentially precludes any close contact – it doesn't take Jung to read into their preference for cold-blooded animals. Snake and lizard owners have a propensity for voyeurism, or at the very least being wallflowers. Plus, there is the whole willingness to *feed another living creature to their pet.* I'm not saying a lizard owner will definitely break your heart, but they're probably not going to spend a lot of time making you feel better about yourself either.

On the exact opposite side, we've got people who own hamsters, gerbils, rabbits, mice – any of the small caged animals. These people care about nothing BUT appearances. While their pets are super cute, they are good for pretty much nothing else. They poop, sleep, occasionally eat each other, and pretty much roll over and die out of boredom. If you are dating someone who owns a hamster or a gerbil, congratulations; you are probably very attractive.

Anyone who owns a baby anything – duckling, piglet, pony, tiger cub – has a major red flag warning flashing overhead. These people give no thought to the future and are unable to consider the consequences of their actions. When Chandler and Joey adopted a baby chick and duck on *Friends*, it wasn't just funny, but also a deep symbolic representation of their emotional immaturity. Notice those pets went away as the characters gave in to adulthood.

But the biggest red flag of them all is a pet bird. If you find out you are dating a bird person, run. Just run. The fundamental truth about these people is that they are perfectly content to keep a creature that is meant to fly trapped inside a tiny cage with no freedom. Even worse, most of them keep that cage somewhere near a window, so the poor bird can see exactly what it is missing every day of its sad little life. Bird people are sadists. Maybe even psychopaths. They will crush your dreams and laugh while doing it. Don't even take the time to make an excuse about an early doctor's appointment the next day – just grab your shit and get the hell out. Now.

Personally, I am a cat person – or, more accurately, a person who attends to cats. Ten years ago I rescued two sisters (Martini and Olive) and between the two of them have been pretty well trained. As potential partners, it is important to know that we cat people tend to also be Cat People – with temperaments very much like those of our feline friends. If dogs are an emotionally needy live-in partner, cats are your asshole roommate. I'm not saying we'll throw up in the middle of the living room if you piss us off, but we are definitely going to live life on our own schedule when we can help it. Cats are independent and often prefer to be alone. Some call this aloof, but I say low-maintenance. It's pretty easy to keep someone happy when they are perfectly content to stare at the same tiny speck on a wall for hours at a time*.

---

*or, as I like to call it, "writing."

Cats are creatures of routine who get openly grumpy when that routine is disturbed – something else to which I, with my obsessive and perfectionist tendencies, can easily relate. We are fastidious, finicky, and often frustrating. To say we are demanding would be an understatement: Martini will cry at me until I move into a position on the couch where she can sleep behind my knees, and if I dare move or stop petting her before she is satisfied, she gives me one of those death stares that I am sure are the reason the Egyptians said, "Better safe than sorry, let's just treat them all like gods." We are too curious for our own good, excessively analytical, and far too prideful. (Have you ever laughed at a cat? It won't look at you for the rest of the day.) All of these things are what make cats less popular than dogs, and what make Cat People more challenging to love.

But to stop at these things would be a disservice. There are such great rewards to be had for those willing to rise to the challenge. As anyone who owns a laser pointer or has had the pleasure of witnessing a cat high on the 'Nip can tell you, we are also completely willing to make fools of ourselves for your amusement. Even better, no matter how often we may get startled and run from random coughs or doorbells, when the chips are down and you need us most, we are fiercely devoted. And if you should be so lucky as to be chosen as our one person, honored and loved above all other mere mammals, rest assured you are going to have our ass in your face every day for the rest of your life. Don't be scared – just rub our belly and we'll fall asleep in no time.

THE LOGARITHM OF LOVE

In 1960, Smokey Robinson's mama dropped some serious truth when she insisted he better Shop Around. Given the decade, Smokey probably assumed her wisdom came from a woman's deep understanding of bargain shopping, but I prefer to think she was simply keeping up with modern trends in mathematics.

Around that same time, numbers guys around the world were turning their attention to a decision-making dilemma they dubbed The Secretary Problem (and occasionally The Marriage Problem). Since the parameters of the problem are applicable to many real-world situations, and since I choose not to indulge the sexist world of the Mad Men era, I like to apply it to dessert and call it the Ice Cream Headache.

Imagine yourself in an ice cream shop facing dozens of flavor options. You have to decide on just one, and ideally you want to choose the very best of all. The rules are simple: first, your choices are finite.* Second, you can sample flavors, but only one at a time, only once each, and you must make a decision immediately upon tasting – choose it, or pass forever. Finally, there are no ties. One is decidedly the best (for you).

---

*It's "31 flavors" not "infinity" flavors.

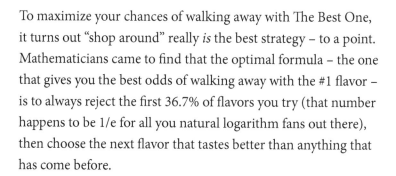
To maximize your chances of walking away with The Best One, it turns out "shop around" really *is* the best strategy – to a point. Mathematicians came to find that the optimal formula – the one that gives you the best odds of walking away with the #1 flavor – is to always reject the first 36.7% of flavors you try (that number happens to be 1/e for all you natural logarithm fans out there), then choose the next flavor that tastes better than anything that has come before.

Say there are nine flavors total. This optimal method means we will taste the first randomly selected three and not choose them, no matter what. The odds of The Best One being in those first three (which means we will definitely NOT win the game) is 33%. The other 67% percent of the time, we still have a chance.

After rejecting the first three, we will choose the very first flavor that tastes better than anything we've had so far. If we happened to taste the *second best* flavor in the first three but *not* The Best One – the odds of which is 25% – we are guaranteed a win. Only The Best One will taste better, so only The Best One will be chosen, no matter how long it takes us to get to it. The remaining 42% of the time, victory depends on when in the subsequent tastings The Best One appears.

When the math is all calculated and done, probability shows that employing this strategy to the Ice Cream Headache results in victory – choosing The Best One – at minimum 37% of the time, which is the best chance possible and far better odds than choosing at random.

Sure, in real life we are free to piss off the ice cream vendors as we test every single flavor over and over until we are either satisfied with our decision or just satisfied, but the parameters of the Ice Cream Headache are remarkably realistic when it comes to dating.

In love, we generally get one shot at evaluation – Burton and Taylor notwithstanding. Likewise, the choice is usually a now-or-never situation. (We may dream of "sampling" a person and then getting to try all the other people too before ultimately deciding, "You were the best," but in reality that usually ends with a "Screw you, I've moved on" and a drink in the face.) Finally, even with today's cacophony of online dating resources, we still have a finite number of candidates.

Applying the lessons of the Ice Cream Headache to a partner search yields some interesting results.

For one, it helps redefine the idea of "success." We usually view situations as win or lose, but mathematics has a third option: draw. Victory in the Ice Cream Headache is walking away with The Best One, but failure isn't everything else; failure only happens if we walk away with a flavor that is *not* the best and thus leave unsatisfied (or at least with that little nagging feeling…). But remember that one-in-three chance The Best One was in the automatically rejected first group? In that case, you, the taster, would never choose any flavor, because nothing would ever meet the requirement of outperforming everything prior. In life terms, that means no partner would ever impress more than the one who was met too early, and the player stays single. It's refreshing (almost as refreshing as ice cream) to think of a single life as being a "draw" rather than a loss, as too many people do.

So at least 37% of the time you win, and 33% of the time you draw. Meaning only 30% of the time (at most) do you wind up committing to something other than The Best One.

More significantly, the Ice Cream Headache validates the practice of living a little before settling down. While we can't know in advance the total *number* of people we will end up dating, we can apply the "reject the first 36.7%" formula to our *time* spent dating for similar results. The average life expectancy of an American woman is 82 years; 77 for American men. If we apply the "discard the first 36.7%" rule, no one should even consider choosing a life partner before age 30 or 28, respectively.

To apply the strategy more specifically to our dating years, let's say no one dates seriously before 15, and we reserve the last 10 years of life for writing memoirs and bowling. That leaves 57 shopping years for women, and 52 for men. Again, if we automatically pass on the first 36.7% of candidates, that translates to 20 years of dating before possibly making a choice (19 for men). Starting at 15, that pushes the start of decision time to our mid-thirties.

Yes, this simplifies things with the premise that potential mates will appear at a steady rate across our dating years (which is now more likely with the internet), but the end result is still valid. Statistically, the optimal strategy over a lifetime for successfully ending up with your ideal flavor is to not get serious about choosing until sometime after 30. Mama was right: you better Shop Around.

Of course, this still doesn't solve the problem of that awesome mocha chip gelato you finally choose deciding *it* doesn't want *you*. But it helps.

LESSON 6
MUSIC
APPRECIATION

DRUMMER WANTED
(TIMING OPTIONAL)

Thought Experiment: Imagine that you are a musician. Maybe you play the guitar, or the piano. For the windier among us, perhaps the harmonica or bagpipes. The instrument doesn't matter; what matters is that *you* are a *musician.*

It is part of who you are, something you have loved and developed since childhood. You practice every day, you study other musicians, read histories of music, and broaden your knowledge as much as possible. Along the way, you find examples of greatness to emulate, and many more examples of not-so-greatness to serve as cautionary tales.

As a solo artist, life is good. Simply making beautiful music is fulfilling and enjoyable. But you also see and envy those truly great bands – The Beatles, The Who, the E-Street gang, and other bands that are more current than the ones I love because of my parents. *Someday,* you think, *I'd love to be a part of something like that, too.*

So now you have a choice. Two roads diverge, as they say. On the first path, you go for it; go find yourself a band. You put up flyers at local music stores and concert venues, you go to gigs to see what musicians are out there, introduce yourself left and right, and tell everyone that your proverbial drummer is indeed wanted.

This is a tried and true method of forming a band, and it *will* work. Every drummer within reach will audition for your band. Some will be terrible, some will be asshats, one might even be Animal (if you're lucky). A couple will probably be good, maybe even great, and one of those will be the drummer who will end up in your band.

Will it make you Nirvana? It's possible, but not likely. Fun is probably a more reasonable model to shoot for, and the odds are you will be just as good as that cool band we all knew in college. Which band? Exactly. Still, you will have your fun.

On the second path, you keep doing what you were doing all along, but turn your band-mate radar on. (Your 'play-dar'?) Practice, play, create, grow; attend shows, find new music, meet people. Do your thing, and all the while be ready for the McCartney to your Lennon, the Grohl to your Cobain, to present himself. When someone's music seems to work really well with yours, suggest a jam session, and explore.

Is it possible you never find that magical partnership? Sure. You could walk right past each other, or they could be serving 5-10 for murdering J.K. Simmons (go watch *Whiplash* if you haven't already), or you could find that ideal counterpart right away – but those scenarios are all outliers. At the very least, you will surely be inspired by several people along the way and grow into a better artist in your own right.

Of course, there *is* technically a third path that can be taken – doing nothing, while you sit around and mope about not being in a band. But that path is clearly marked Dead End.

So, of the two viable options, which road do you choose? Neither one is better than the other, they just lead to different places and feature different views. Is your primary goal to be part of a band, or to prepare yourself for great collaboration when the opportunity knocks?

We are each our own instrument. Our lives are our music. Some people seek their band, find it, and it is good. Others hone their craft, watching for potential partners along the way, and have a fulfilling journey regardless.

The choice is personal. (So, stop asking why I'm not on OK Cupid, Mom – but do remind me to look up from the music once in a while.)

FULL-FRONTAL NERDITY 102: RELATIONSHIPS

CHEMISTRY

A PERIODIC FABLE OF ELEMENTS

Anyone who has ever been a girl scout knows that new friends are silver and old ones are gold. This makes perfect sense. Both metals are highly malleable, strong, flexible, and of significant weight and substance. All friendships should have those qualities. But silver is also lighter, shinier, and a better conductor of both heat and electricity; new things are always more exciting than old ones.

Relating friendships to metals is especially apt when you consider the properties of non-metals. Non-metals are not shiny, are generally poor conductors of energy, are brittle (if solid at all), and most tellingly become transparent when stretched thin (whereas metals remain opaque). We all have those people in our lives who seem like friends but suddenly disappear when the pressure is on. Many of them are also giant gas bags – or at the very least full of hot air.

So our friends are precious metals and the rest are not. But surely there are more types of friendship than just "new" and "old." In my experience, the flavors of friendship are as distinctive and varied as the elements themselves.

Iron, for instance, has the most stable nucleus of all the metals, and its configuration of electrons makes it highly magnetic. A stable core with a strong attraction? Sounds like a life-long best friendship to me. I'm talking about those people you meet in childhood who, no matter the moves, school changes, separate adventures, or life developments, stay on your speed dial through it all. You may not talk to these friends every day, but you could if you needed to, and that's what matters. Iron may not be as pretty or shiny as gold and silver, but it makes a hell of a lot better support beam. If you're lucky enough to have an Iron friendship in your lifetime, as I am, it will hold you up through the strongest winds, floods, and earthquakes.

Speaking of support, a different friend of mine once commented that it is never fair to expect anyone to be supportive all the time, because no one person ever will be. Never mind that her argument in the moment was an attempted excuse for not giving me a ride to the airport, she was and remains wrong because I know personally that those people and those bonds do exist. These friends, who will always say yes if it is physically possible to help you, are platinum, which is rare and resists corrosion of any kind – even airport pickups. If you are lucky enough to have something platinum, any fashionista can tell you that it is the only accessory you need.

Long-distance friendships are copper; they can be stretched very thin and yet remain incredibly strong and are excellent conductors of energy – which they have to be to sustain the necessary work involved. Still, we must be careful with these friendships. Copper can tarnish easily, probably because sarcasm doesn't translate well over email. Emojis and gifs can only do so much – call your long-distance friends once in a while!

On the other end of the spectrum from copper are titanium friendships, which conduct very little electricity or heat but have a high strength-to-weight ratio. They can sustain a lot with very little substance. These are our favorite acquaintances, or our "outer circle" – the people we don't actively seek out, but always enjoy when we find ourselves in their company. In today's virtual world, many of our friendships are titanium, which may sound cynical but isn't. Titanium can be just as attractive as platinum, silver, or gold, and if every accessory we had was a heavy metal, we'd be dragged down by the weight of it. These friendships are a valuable resource for the day-to-day, less serious moments in our lives.

It is the "Facebook friendships" that are cheap aluminum. Aluminum is the most abundant metal on the planet, which is how that jackass from high school can have several thousand Instagram followers, and it resists corrosion – something far easier to do when you can just "mute" a person any time they get a little unpleasant. Much like any social media platform or online comments section, aluminum is an excellent conductor of heat, and the extreme malleability of aluminum is why we can crumple it up and toss it as soon as it has served its purpose. The internet: best for catching drips, roasting corny husks, and baking couch potatoes.

Beware of lead friends, who do nothing but weigh you down, and of frenemies, who are made of whatever Sauron used for the One Ring. But do take up tin friendships: gay-straight bonds, or any communion between differing sexual orientations. And no, these relationships are not tin just because the Tin Man was totally a friend of Dorothy, but because tin is immensely useful and valuable (for example, if you need to feed a traveling army) while still presenting some potential hazards. On the plus side, tin is resistant to heat and moisture, and this freedom from any sexual potential can allow for much deeper emotional intimacy. Tin is also ductile, making it resistant to shock— which is good for when these friendships result in eye-opening, mind-expanding conversations. But at the same time, tin can be polished to a shine much greater than its natural state and is often used as a protective coating over other metals. So be careful – there is a reason it took Will and Grace decades (and still counting) to find other relationships.

Which brings us to those friendships that do have the complication of extra attraction between the two parties. Harry and Sally demonstrated quite clearly that men and women can be friends, but it is also true that romantic attractions change the chemical makeup of things.

Mercury relationships are when the attraction is one sided, and for the other side nothing will ever progress beyond friendship. As a metal, mercury is not a good conductor of heat (though certainly *is* a good conductor of electricity – for one person at least), is liquid, and is slippery; likewise, navigating a romantic imbalance in a relationship can be quite tricky. That is not to say it's impossible, but it takes a delicate and deliberate touch – and probably some kid gloves. Also, like mercury, an over-abundance of these friendships in your diet can be toxic.

The flip side of mercury friendships is one where two people were once romantically involved but are no longer. If the romantic portion of the relationship has truly run its course for both parties, an incredibly strong bond can result. These friendships are tungsten, which is rare and extremely hard. Tungsten has the highest melting point of all the metals (it takes a lot to destroy it after all that history) but can also be brittle – especially if someone's new partner is a jealous person.

But if the romantic relationship ended before one party was ready for it to be over, that's where we move away from metals into metalloids. Metalloid relationships can be mistaken for friendships (especially by the person who is done with the romance), but they are not really. Trying to be friends with an ex who broke your heart may seem essential, may appear desirable, and may even be prescribed as a bit of healthy medicine, but in truth is a situation that is brittle, toxic, and easily fatal. Exactly like the metalloid arsenic. Which, not coincidentally, is an element commonly used in pyrotechnics. Sparks fly; people cry; dreams die.

There is some hope, though. When arsenic is added to copper (distance), the result can turn out to be bronze – a strong, hard metal from which great art can be cast. So the next time you need help not texting that person who recently left you broken hearted, consider going to an art museum instead; admire the bronzes and look to the future with hope.

POETRY

APRIL FOOL

The month of April during my sophomore year of college was dubbed by my roommate "The Month of Doom." In those few weeks, several *major* relationships within the Harvard Band came crashing down, and she noted that a similar string of breakups had occurred in April of our freshman year, too. Snuggled comfortably in the warmth of her *new* relationship, she simply shrugged and noted that there "must be something in the air." Since one of the relationships that had so recently disintegrated had been *mine*, and since the observation was essentially her only response to my devastation, I didn't appreciate the sentiment all that much at the time. Looking back, though, she was completely right.

> *April is the cruelest month, breeding*
> *Lilacs out of the dead land, mixing*
> *Memory and desire, stirring*
> *Dull roots with spring rain.*

> —*T. S. Eliot, "The Waste Land"*

April is many things – including National Poetry Month – but at its heart it is a month of transition and change; it is a month when things end, and other things begin. It is the Spring from which hope springs eternally, which can be cruel as it reminds us of the crushed hopes of Springs past. But don't let Mr. Eliot convince you it is a waste of energy – without a new hope, where would we be?*

Historically, April has seen the start of the American Revolution, the first shots of the American Civil War, the first Olympics in over 1500 years, and the first space shuttle mission. It has seen endings such as the *last* shots of the Civil War, the official end to slavery (with the Civil Rights Bill of 1866), the assassination of Martin Luther King Jr., and the spiritual end to apartheid with the election of Nelson Mandela. As for transition, it has brought us several events that have literally shaken us to the core, including the explosion aboard Apollo 13, the sinking of the Titanic, and the 1906 San Francisco earthquake. April is also the birth *and* death month of one William Shakespeare.

> *Oh, how this spring of love resembleth*
> *The uncertain glory of an April Day;*
> *Which now shows all the beauty of the sun,*
> *And by and by a cloud takes all away.*
>
> —*William Shakespeare, Two Gentlemen of Verona*

Is it any wonder that so many relationships burst forth and die in this tumultuous spring month? That April back in sophomore year saw the end of my relationship with my first love. But the April before it had brought our first date: a romantic

---

*We'd be without Princess Leia, for one, and that's unacceptable.

walk on a perfect spring night, a pause on a bridge spanning the Charles River, a lunar eclipse, and a fumbling first kiss.

> *The April winds are magical,*
> *And thrill out tuneful frames;*
> *The garden walks are passional,*
> *To bachelors and dames.*
>
> —*Ralph Waldo Emerson, "April"*

It was April again a couple of years later when I ventured to England to visit my star-crossed soul mate. We spent a week wandering through gardens, exploring museums, getting lost on beaches and in woods, and sharing long nights of conversation in cramped single beds. At the end of that trip, we realized that life (my work, his school) was directing us both toward Los Angeles, where we would be in the same time zone for the first time in our history. It was either the beginning of forever, or the end of someday. He met his wife the day after I left, and our relationship was never close again, but I wouldn't give up that week for all the happiness in the world. To me, at the time, it *was* all the happiness in the world.

> *April comes in like an idiot, babbling and strewing flowers.*
>
> —*Edna St. Vincent Millay, "Spring"*

A few Aprils after that, I entered my first (and, so far, only) romantic cohabitation. Sure, part of the reason I agreed to the scenario was because I *knew* I would *never* marry him in the long run (that made it safe, you see, because I was too young to be heading down that road), and sure, it was doomed from the start, but that didn't stop us from being excited, even downright giddy at the idea of playing house for the first time. That, and saving major bank on the split rent. And it doesn't mean it wasn't a worthwhile experiment.

> *April is a promise that May is bound to keep.*
>
> —*Hal Borland (New York Times editorialist)*

Then again, our giddiness at living together also didn't stop *him* from deciding only two months later to pack it in and move back to the other side of the country. It took him a full year to actually leave, and the word awkward doesn't even begin to describe what that year was like, but I came away with the furnished, rent -controlled apartment. Totally worth it.

> *April, April,*
> *Laugh thy girlish laughter,*
> *Then, the moment after,*
> *Weep thy girlish tears.*
>
> —*Sir William Watson, "April"*

Nowadays, the month of April brings the Coachella music festival, which for me will forever be associated with saying goodbye to my second great love. One April, around the time Gnarls Barkley was a more familiar name than CeeLo Green, I realized I was in love with him and he realized he wasn't with me. He went off to the desert swearing we would always be friends, and in every way except for the physical, he never came back.

> *The sun was warm, but the wind was chill,*
> *You know how it is with an April day*
>
> —*Robert Frost, "Two Tramps in Mud Time"*

More recently, in an April only a couple of years ago, I had finally defrosted my heart and opened it again. I started the month by seeing my boyfriend off on his three-week European adventure (an assignment for work). We vowed to Skype every couple of days; he took me on video tours of his London neighborhood; I tucked a few romantic notes into his luggage to be discovered over time (a practice that had become our custom). But through it all, I could tell that he was growing distant, the solo trip rekindling his wanderlust and loner spirit. The omens of that April fulfilled their promise when he returned in May. We were all over by the end of June.

> *Sweet April showers*
> *Do bring May flowers*
>
> —*Thomas Tusser, "500 Points of Good Husbandry"*

The important thing to remember is that endings are also the prologues to beginnings. The sad spring showers *do* feed the growing flowers, and every one of my tumultuous Aprils have carried me forward to some other new adventure. No ending is ever the end of everything, except possibly one particularly grim theory about the universe collapsing on itself in a reverse Big Bang. But apart from *that* happening, the important thing is to keep moving forward.

I have no idea what the next April will bring; I would rather it be the start of something than the end – unless it is the end of something bad. But no matter what, I hope that I will dive in with abandon, as I have so many Aprils in the past. Because in the end...

> *...the first of April is the day we remember what we are the other 364 days of the year.*
>
> —*Mark Twain*

I will always be an April fool.

HOW DO I LOVE ME? (LET ME COUNT THE WAYS)

Narcissus didn't stand a chance. All he had to do to live a long and healthy life was avoid reflective surfaces, yet there he sat, in his prime, wasting away on the edge of a lake. Seems pretty weak – except it was inevitable. While he certainly wasn't a perfect man, Narcissus did have a really, *really* good-looking reflection.

It is well documented that my heart and I have an unhealthy affinity for narcissists. This is clearly not good for me, as evidenced by the fact that my most successful relationships thus far have been with my two dependent cats and a '96 Toyota, but I am certainly not alone in my addiction. I have tried to kick the habit time and again, but I keep running into the same snag: the problem with many narcissists is that there is actually a lot of awesomeness there to adore.

The original Narcissus was literally part god. He was the love child of the river god Cephisus and a sexy nymph named Lyriope, so his esteem for his own physique was 100% legit. Even Apollo – the real-deal god, not the pilot from *Battlestar*

Galactica, though I personally would take either – was infatuated because Narcissus was so frakking pretty. While I have never had the pleasure of a romantic entanglement with such an exceptional beauty, experience has taught me that every narcissist has some remarkable trait that makes him worthy of affection – his own as well as mine.

(Of course, there are also plenty of folks with a completely unfounded esteem for their own greatness, but we should label them accurately as what they really are: delusional.)

Like a Jane Goodall of the Ego jungle, my years in the field have brought me vast knowledge of these cold yet fascinating creatures. They are not all alike, but they are all capable of driving a lover to despair. In hopes of saving even one future Aminias – the Narcissus admirer who kills himself in the Greek version of the myth – or Echo – who in Ovid's telling retreats to the mountains to end her days in lovelorn solitude – I feel obligated to share my research with the world.

Within the Genus *Narcissa* I have so far categorized three distinct Species: the Passionate Artist, the Depressed Intellectual, and the King of the Room. Which makes me Dorothy in a manic pixie mumblecore version of *The Wizard of Oz.*

Artiste Passio is the most classic species of narcissist. This guy is all about his talent, which only makes him increasingly talented. I have pined for brilliant writers, hilarious performers, and more musicians* than I care to admit, but regardless of medium, the

---

*okay, bass players

outcome is the same: there is no room for anything but The Craft. Sure, these Artists love the attention, the admiration, and the praise we shower on them, but that is all they love. From whom the praise flows is irrelevant – unless that whom happens to have financial backing. Shutting off the affection faucet will often get the Artist's attention (they might even take steps to keep it flowing freely), but do not mistake a love of being loved for actual love of the lover. We are merely faces in their adoring throng.

A more controversial species is the *Literati Depresso* – not because it is controversial to be depressed (heck, it is practically vogue these days), but because calling a depressed person a narcissist isn't exactly PC. I don't care; while it is certainly not the case that all depressed people are narcissistic, I have had enough relationships with the more Tormented variety of depressives – who can suffer under everything from a chemical imbalance to Woody Allen – to know that a certain amount of self-obsession is needed to maintain that level of inner torment. It takes impressive focus and mental agility to see every interaction as a reflection on themselves, analyze all new information in terms of how it impacts their life, and suspect that every personal thought might hold the secret to their impossible existence. No question, these Eeyores have remarkable brains, but rest assured there is no capacity reserved for wondering how *we* might be feeling today. (Unless it is how we are feeling about them…)

Rex Locus is the third and most insidious species of narcissist – the King of the Room. This is the guy with Personality.

Mr. Awesome. His defining characteristic is that people love him, but the problem is his lack of ability – or possibly courage – to sincerely love anyone in return. Narcissus loved that Echo followed him everywhere, so he called out that she should show herself; when she rushed out of hiding and hugged him, he recoiled at the intimacy and literally shoved her aside. The King of the Room does the same. Their 'why' will vary from one to the next – they're a loner, they're a rebel, we aren't perfect, we're too perfect – but it will always be some version of, "Uncertainty and vulnerability scare me! So…. I'm gonna go meet a room full of new people now." Like sharks they keep moving forward, leaving us to flounder in their wake.

Still, we chase these narcissists time and again, keep Echoing their greatness, and we probably always will. Pain fades over time, but Talent, Intelligence, and Charm remain potent drugs. Narcissus didn't stand a chance against his own beauty; how can we Echos be expected to resist?

LESSON 10
PULP LITERATURE
LOIS LAME

When I was little, Nancy Drew was my hero. My mom had
inherited her mom's collection of the original mysteries,
and they in turn became mine. Those books were my most
prized possessions, and I read all of them more times than I
can count. I also looked up to Princess Leia (kicking ass with
fantastic hair), to Dorothy Gale (loyalty to pets *and* a taste for
adventure), and to Miss Piggy (who taught me self-esteem). But
the woman I wanted to *be* was Lois Lane.

From the slim pickings of female role models in comics, Lois
was queen. Sure, Wonder Woman was cool, what with the
whole Amazonian goddess thing, but Lynda Carter's stunning
beauty – and ridiculous twirling – made her completely
unrelatable to me. Also, even my naïve pre-teen sensibilities
understood the sexism inherent in a female superhero who
wears impractically-tiny outfits, is vulnerable without her
jewelry, and carries a magic rope that allows her to know what
any man is thinking.

Catwoman was out of the question because, much as I love cats,
I was way too goody-goody to admire a criminal, and Batgirl
just made me think about how much I'd rather be at a baseball
game. (As a DC Comics kid, I didn't have the pleasure of
meeting MJ or Rogue until much later.) Lois Lane was my girl.

I *loved* her. She was smart (except for the whole glasses/no glasses thing) and accomplished, a career woman with too much ambition to care about fashion trends or fads (a freedom I longed for as an uncool child); Lois didn't just hang with the boys, she surpassed them. Plus, Margot Kidder portrayed her as also clumsy and bad at spelling – two things with which I could relate on a deeply personal level. Lois was brave and curious and willing to be a little bad for the greater good, and on top of all that, *Superman loved her.*

It kind of makes me want to hurl now, but I am pretty sure the reason I loved Lois Lane the most was because her boyfriend was Superman. My younger self operated under the misconception that the greatest proof of a girl's awesomeness was the quality of man who loved her, and Lois was chosen by the greatest man on the planet. Literally. This reasoning was no less lame than the modern trend of male filmmakers who demonstrate the appeal of their thinly-veiled protagonist stand-ins by giving them the inexplicable (and usually unearned) attentions of a manic pixie dream girl or Katherine Heigl*.

I'm not sure which is worse: realizing my own logic was so messed up as a kid or realizing that so many adult men still think like a 13-year-old girl.

Admitting my own fault wasn't nearly as hard, though, as coming to terms with the major disappointment of Lois herself. It didn't happen until college, when I met my own Superman and dove headfirst into a relationship with him, finally living

*Judd Apatow

the dream. We were together for about three years, and he is, to this day, one of the best and dearest people in my life. But our relationship forced me to face a harsh truth: being Superman's girlfriend really *sucks*.

Superman is, above all else, a hero. His primary objective is to be of use, no matter how small the problem. A not-so-healthy blend of Catholicism and Geekery had given my Superman similar aims, and while he couldn't fly he could certainly help carry a couch or give you a ride whenever you needed it. The thing is, being helpful *always* came first – above other things like being on time, making it to dinner, or answering phone calls and emails (we didn't have texts yet, but if we did, I am sure he would have ignored those too).

A lot of fun was had on the show *Lois & Clark* with scenarios where Clark/Superman would miss an anniversary celebration and get away with it because he was stopping a nuclear war or something, but I learned to feel Lois's pain very quickly. On the one hand, you can't be mad at a guy for missing dinner (or being late) because he was stopping global destruction (or bringing a sick friend soup). But on the other hand – dammit, he could have taken a second to call (or gone to get the soup after meeting you).

I wasted hours trying to articulate how it is bad enough to make everyone a priority (which then makes nobody a priority), but far worse to make your girlfriend a *lower* priority because she already loves you. Is a message saying, "Hey, I'm not dead, I just stopped to help a guy with a flat" too much to ask? But there is simply no way to fight with Superman without looking like the jerk yourself; *everyone* loves him – and they should, because he probably helped them move that one time.

Add to all this the inherent condescension that comes with Superman's impossible moral standards for himself – he is a Christ figure, after all – and the relationship becomes an exercise in balancing self-hate with anger. I was mad at the guy who was pure of intention and heart, which made me hate myself; I felt ashamed for wanting to just have fun sometimes instead of helping with something when we technically could; and I raged at him for *not* expecting me, a mere mortal, to put being helpful first. (There is a reason "holier than thou" is an insult rather than a compliment.) In short: it was unhealthy.

Maybe I am just not a good enough person to be Superman's girlfriend, but I am pretty sure the real truth is that I am no longer dumb enough. Lois Lane *did* get shafted in that relationship (though not literally, because his Super Sperm would have made her uterus explode). He left her hanging way more than he showed up (unless she was literally hanging from a ledge), he *never* gave her the courtesy of a note or a phone call (apparently, he was not Super enough to actually *use* the phone while changing), and by never putting their relationship first he made her feel terrible every time *she* did.

It took me about three years to accept that this scenario was unsustainable. Lois Lane, on the other hand, still hasn't figured it out.

LESSON 11
ANALYTICS

POKER FACE (THAT'S WHAT SHE SAID)

In 2012, I wrote a romantic dark comedy about a girl who starts an underground casino on the Princeton campus in order to pay for her suddenly scholarship-less senior year. Since the only personal experience I have with gambling is playing "Vegas rules" solitaire on my computer when I'm procrastinating, I had to do quite a bit of research before I could write it. One of my favorite discoveries came when reading about the psychology of the greatest poker players, because it changed the way I chose to evaluate my love life.

In poker, as in much of life, there are four possible outcomes every time we play a hand: we can play well and win (yay!); we can play poorly and lose (boo!); we can play poorly and win anyway (yay!); or we can play well and still lose (double boo!). Most of us – mere humans that we are – are emotional creatures, or what Lord Voldemort would call "weak." While Voldy's assessment is a tad harsh, it *is* true that our emotional dominance tends to result in reactions like those of the parenthetical cheerleader above (Mr. "Yay! Boo! Yay!"). We focus primarily on results – winning is good, losing is bad.

But *some* people are ruled more by logic instead – Sherlock Holmes, the main character on *Bones*, and Mr. Spock to name a few. These people would have very different reactions to the four possible outcomes, because they don't focus on results as much as process when judging performance. Good poker players (and good learners too, by the way) know that long-term success demands that they learn to think this way – to be more Spock than jock – and they have the experience and maturity to "make it so."*

A professional poker player understands that sometimes, luck happens. Sometimes, you play the odds perfectly, and read an opponent just right, but he still draws that *one* improbable card that gives him the *one* hand that can beat you. Yes, this hand is lost, but what matters most is that it was played well. The successful poker player walks away from this situation satisfied, and would be similarly *displeased* if the roles had been reversed and *she* had won on a lucky card rather than skilled play.

Daft Punk may be up all night to get lucky, but the best poker players are up all night to hone their craft.

Empirically, I know this to be the path to success. I tell my LSAT students relentlessly, because I have seen it bear out time and again: focus on the process instead of the score, and not only will you be happier, you will also ultimately see much better scores. It is logic. It is proven. It is also much easier said than done.

---

*Yeah, yeah, I know that's Picard's line.

For example, when I tell people about my romantic travails from one particularly eventful year in my past, most of them immediately want to give me a hug, buy me a cookie, and remind me that which does not kill us makes us stronger. I'm not gonna lie – it was an emotionally rough year. But *I* look at the year as a success, because it is also the year I finally learned to start looking at the world with the eye of my inner poker player. Yes, I had two relationships end in one year, and yes, both times it was because he chose to be alone rather than be with me. I could have easily looked at that, seen the final score of two defeats, and decided to try being a different person. But instead, I chose to not let the outcomes bother me. Sometimes, two people just aren't meant to be together – and boy, did I not belong with either of those people. Instead, I now chose to focus on how I handled things once that truth was known.

Neither of the two men involved in these romances was capable of sustaining a long-term relationship. The first was a true loner; he loved me, but after a year his wanderlust started making him more and more distant. When this became too apparent to ignore – as did the fact that he was never going to own up to it on his own – I sat him down and told him to figure out what he wanted. If it was me, fantastic, I was all in; but if it wasn't, he needed to go so I could find a man who did want me. He decided what he wanted was to leave, and yeah, it was heartbreaking, but for the first time in my life I had handled a romantic entanglement with complete maturity and strength. *That* was a huge amount of solace. Even though I lost the relationship, I walked away with pride because of my good play – and hoped to continue such behavior in the future.

Naturally, my handling of the next guy was a complete disaster. He was self-absorbed, closed off, and a really good liar (one of my Passionate Artist narcissists). Even though, in the few short months we were together, my inner voice kept screaming, "Get out! You deserve better than this!" like Daniel Kaluuya I chose to believe him every time he begged for patience and forgiveness. (I had clearly not mastered Bayesian reasoning.) My last capitulation – an agreement *at his request* to pause, let the holidays pass, and regroup after life was calmer and heads were clearer – was rewarded with an abrupt break-up speech two days later, while we were literally en route from one Christmas party to another. It really couldn't have ended dumber.

Still, even though in the immediate sense that last relationship was more of a win than a loss (being single was so much better than being with him), I seethe with shame every time I look back at it because I really could not have played it worse. Well, okay, I could have "accidentally" gotten pregnant by him to appease my biological clock – *THAT* would have been worse. But you get my point. Any outcome based on bad play is far less desirable than even a loss after good.

Poker mentality is a refreshing alternative to our usual results-based evaluations. It is especially vital for one's sanity when taking the life or career path less traveled. Sure, it's a little annoying that to my friends on the outside looking in I appear far more upset about (and thus attached to) the jerk than the guy I actually loved, but that's on them for making assumptions. I'll take my healthier mental state any day.

Of course, it is still harder to practice than to preach. Not only do we have to learn to focus on process over outcome in the face of a culture that overwhelmingly cares about results, but we also have to learn to trust our own evaluation of that process. This is especially hard in an imperfect and uncertain world, where it is often difficult to distinguish bad luck from bad strategy. Did this relationship or project fail because it just wasn't meant to be, or because there is something wrong with my selection process? Most of the time, it's probably a little bit of both.

But just because something is hard doesn't mean it isn't worth doing. We just need to practice. The more experience we collect, the easier it will become to judge our process and then to trust that judgment. Start small (my oven timer broke and the cookies burned, but the batter tasted great, so that's still good), work up to the bigger things (sure, my kid's a rocket scientist, but what matters is that I taught her to be *nice* to people, yay me), and counteract inherent uncertainty with self-forgiveness.

If we focus on the method instead of the goal, we will find far more pleasure in the process, and ultimately achieve greater outcomes than we ever imagined. (That's what she said.)

LESSON 12
PHILOSOPHY

CE N'EST PAS UNE PIÈCE

Love is a curious paradox; one no one can explain. *Who understands the secrets of the reaping of the grain? Who understands why spring is born out of winter's laboring pain, or why we all must die a bit before we grow again?*

With all due respect to *The Fantasticks* (from which the above lines are lyrics), I don't generally like to "Try to Remember" the month of September, as the song implores us to do. For one thing, that play originally starred Jerry Orbach, and after a lifetime of *Law & Order*, *Dirty Dancing*, and *Beauty & the Beast* fandom, I am still depressed that cancer took him from us. Also, one particular September was once very rough on my heart.

Besides, *The Fantasticks* is a play where two dads arrange for an old dude to attempt the rape of one dad's daughter so the other dad's son can save her and fall in love. That's messed up.

(Yet it is a truly fantastic play – how paradoxical.)

Love *is* a curious paradox, though. The play isn't wrong. We can only find it when we aren't looking for it, we have to fail at it in order to succeed, and it is hardest to lose when we didn't need it in the first place.

Sartre (the original Debbie Downer) nailed the paradoxical truth about love in his epic and depressing work *Being and Nothingness*, where he observed that love is so vital to us and we so fear losing it that we desire to control the will of our beloved; we wish we could guarantee their love in return. Yet love is only valuable when freely given by another person, so the moment we got our wish and could secure said love would be the moment that love lost all meaning.*

The very thing that makes love terrifying – the fact that it can be lost or not returned and that feels like it might kill us – is the only thing that makes it worth seeking.

Breakups are also paradoxical. A love that matters is thusly worth fighting for, but in fighting we risk removing the value entirely. Still, the fight itself is necessary.

A long time ago, when I was young(er) and dumb(er), I got mad at my boyfriend for not doing the dishes while I was at work. He pointed out that I had not asked him to do the dishes; had he known, he probably would have. Or, let's be honest, he probably still wouldn't have, but at least then I'd have had every right to be angry. As it was, I couldn't blame him for not satisfying an expectation I had never vocalized. Grubby dishes aside, he was completely right.

---

*Sartre said it in a far more complex and French way, with sad music and cigarettes.

Now, I speak up whenever I want something. Including – and especially – when that something is a someone.

When a love matters, it is important to tell the person they matter. It is important to say out loud what we want, to give voice to all of the good that stands to be lost, and to politely point out that by leaving or hiding from love this person is making a terrible mistake.

But somewhere in the middle of the argument, in the middle of the tears, the declarations of "we're awesome" and "that's no reason to throw it all away" there is also that little voice inside speaking the truth we don't want to acknowledge. The one that knows the paradox cannot be resolved. That traitorous logician asking, "What good is a love I talked someone into?"

To win the fight and keep the relationship would be to simultaneously lose the value of the love. Yet to not fight would mean it never really mattered in the first place. And round and round it goes… the following statement is true; the previous statement is false… this sentence is not here.

I guess the trick is to fight for what we want and also have the nerve to never get it.

I do not know the answer; I only know it's true. I hurt them for that reason, and myself a little bit too.

(It really is a Fantastick play. Go see it.)

FULL-FRONTAL NERDITY 103: LIFE (STRIVING)

LESSON 13
PHYSICS

QUANTUM LEAPING

Not too long ago, a friend and I were discussing the defining challenges we humans all face over the course of each decade of life. You know… how, for the first ten years, life is all about mastering the basics, like walking, talking, and not soiling yourself; in the next ten years, the challenge is learning to navigate social situations and surviving high school (again, without soiling yourself); and, in your twenties, the struggle is about coming to understand that you have *not* actually figured it all out and that you really are, in fact, still kind of a shit. Nearing the end of our thirties, my friend and I decided that the major lesson we have spent the last decade fighting to learn is how to rise to the challenge of letting it all go – how to not worry so much about how we might possibly be perceived or what we're "supposed" to think or feel, and instead just live the life we want to live, as the person we really are.

Within reason, of course. We're not talking about ignoring the existence of consequences or other people and running willy-nilly around the planet in a hedonistic dance of Trumpian privilege. Rather, we were talking about the quest to remain a solid, responsible member of society while also moving freely outside the rigidity of its unhelpful expectations.

This is a challenge facing all people, but one that is significantly harder for women, because for us the expectations are far more rigid and far less helpful. Our fearless leader, Barbara Streisand, summed it up nicely when, after a decade and a half spent pushing the rock that was *Yentl* up the Hollywood Hills only to be vilified for it, she said, "Why is it men are permitted to be obsessed about their work, but women are only permitted to be obsessed about men?" At my first job after college, I can remember the frustration of feeling this double standard but not being able to define it. When I defended one of my ideas in a meeting, I was invariably chided for "taking things personally," while my male colleagues who did the same were praised as "passionate" and "assertive." No matter how I tried to find a different way to word things, or a different tone to speak in, the results remained the same: when they did it, it was commendable behavior, but when I did it I was being difficult. The societal expectations set for women are more defined, less forgiving, and outline a far smaller space than the relatively boundless landscapes available to men – and it really doesn't help that random estrogen surges occasionally make us cry for no discernable reason at all.

So my friend and I started talking about how often we let the judgment of society (or even the potential judgment) have more say in our behavior than our own desires. Do *I want* to be starting a family? No, but I feel like I should. Do *I want* to cut this negative person out of my life? Yes, but I am afraid they will hate me. Do *I want* to tell this story or voice this opinion? Yes, but what if they call me a bitch? Even with Tina Fey declaring "bitch is the new black" in 2008, that one still hurts. But we need to stop letting ourselves be so limited. Yes, we should remain aware and considerate of other humans' existence (put down that tiki torch), but also breathe free and allow ourselves to reach our full potential. In other words, we need to unleash our inner quantum.

The theory of quantum mechanics exists because over the years scientists have come to understand that, at the most fundamental levels, particles operate in far more interesting and liberated ways than boring solid objects do in the real world. The marquee headline being that atomic particles can and do exist in two states at once. Why? Because of quantum. Duh.

Okay, to be a little more specific, our basic building blocks of matter – electrons, photons, quarks and such – have been proven by various geniuses to be both particles and waves. That means that they are both solid "quants" that are a contained package of energy/mass that moves from one state to another like walking up a flight of stairs, and flowing waves that move continuously from one state to another as if on skis. If this sounds confusing and impossible, then welcome to the party – Einstein, Bohr, Feynman, Heisenberg, and Schrodinger have been here for a while and have already finished off the good wine – but it's essentially the difference between playing a musical scale on a piano where each of the notes are distinct keys (quants) and sliding through a musical scale on a trombone (waves).

Regardless of why or how, the big problem for many scientists (and other logical types) is the idea that there are separate rules

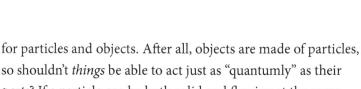

for particles and objects. After all, objects are made of particles, so shouldn't *things* be able to act just as "quantumly" as their *parts*? If a particle can be both solid and flowing at the same time, why can't I? That little syllogism is probably why so many of us – you too, don't pretend – believe deep in our bones that quantum tunneling, teleportation, time travel, and all those sci-fi fantasies *must* be possible.

One of these contemporary scientists, Aaron O'Connell, was so certain the logic must follow that he became the first person to actually get a solid object to be in two places (or states) at once. No kidding. For a fully respectable explanation of his break-through, check out O'Connell's 2011 TED talk (*Making Sense of a Visible Quantum Object*), but for now let me hit you with the highlights. To achieve his result, O'Connell had to figure out what it takes for a physical object to "unleash its inner quantum"* The answer tuned out to be… nothing.

Literally nothing, in this case. O'Connell created a tiny piece of metal that he then suspended over a void in a containment device that allowed him to remove all light, sound, and air, and lower the temperature to just above absolute zero. When completely free of any interference, the tiny object began to "breathe." More precisely, they found that it was both still and vibrating simultaneously – which means its various particles were stationary and yet flowing like Daveed Diggs at the same time. Two states, one object. Whoa.

---

*my silliness, not his.

The analogy O'Connell uses to explain his experiment is an elevator. As solid objects, we basically live life in a crowded elevator, with lots of other things to keep us company and keep us acting "normal." In essence, this is the same idea as the principle of quantum physics underlying the Schrodinger's Cat experiment – that the act of observation forces a thing with multiple possible states into one observable reality. The other people in the elevator are observers, so we remain in our solid, normal state, despite our quantum potential. But just like you and I are way more likely to get jiggy with the Muzak when there are no other passengers or visible security cameras (I can't be the only one), solid objects are more likely to behave quantum mechanically when they are alone.

On a practical level, I am pretty sure that this means Aaron O'Connell has proven the show *Quantum Leap* to be entirely accurate, except for the fact that Sam Beckett could see, hear, breathe, and didn't boil to death in a freezing vacuum. On a broader level, though, his discovery is significant because it reinforces the idea that the more we can kick out of the elevators that are our heads, the closer we can come to operating at our full potential.

For regular humans like us, it is a matter of shutting out the light of all the eyes that might be watching and judging, banishing the sound of our own doubt, pride and insecurity, ignoring the winds of both criticism and praise, and not feeling the heat of embarrassment or fear. If we can boot all of that interference out of our head space, maybe we can finally start to live quantumly – both remaining solid (the person we are, with the qualities and in the reality we cannot change) and at the same time flowing freely (quantum leaping like fools to the Muzak of our souls).

Or, maybe we'll just invent time travel, which would be pretty cool too. Oh, boy!

LESSON 14
SEMANTICS

TO DREAM THE IMPROBABLE DREAM

Where exactly is the line between ambition and masochism, and what are the signs that one has crossed over it without noticing? On dark days, like when I miss out on the chance to land an English Prince or can't afford a ticket to Hamilton or am reminded by my body that yet another egg has gone unfertilized, I often ask this question. It was probably always there to some degree, but around age 33 it really started to knock loudly on my brain, and often. Probably because once you reach that "I've outlived Jesus/Hamlet/Garp" moment, it is only natural to take a hard look at what you have accomplished so far. Sacrificed yourself for humanity yet? No? How about avenged your father's death? At least written enough to anger a movement and get assassinated?

Ambition – n. 1: the desire to achieve a particular end; 2: an ardent desire for rank, fame, or power.

The only positions of rank I have ever striven for or achieved are that of first lieutenant of the marching band and captain of the high school math team, and I long ago concluded that any level of fame beyond just enough name recognition to get a good dinner reservation would make me miserable. But still, I have always been an ambitious person. Even without Winston

Churchill or an Uncle Ben* in my life, it was clear to me that "with great power comes great responsibility." Or, in other words, that when your parents give you genetic gifts, you use them.

What I've never quite been able to settle on is the degree to which this obligation to use talent should dictate life decisions. I read once that one of my favorite baseball players, Nomar Garciaparra, loved soccer the most, but played baseball because he was so good at it and his dad wanted him to. Was that the right decision? It certainly brought career success and a lot of joy to the world – I enjoyed the hell out of his shirtless Sports Illustrated cover photo – but it makes me a little sad to think he didn't love the game as much as something else.

In my junior year of college, the campus was abuzz with news of a freshman girl from India who had been recruited by the school in large part because she was six-foot-eight and good at basketball. (How could she not be, at that height?) Upon arrival, she told the college she would not be playing basket-ball so she could focus on getting the most out of her Harvard education. I found myself behind her in line for milk one day, and as I watched her unfold from using the dispenser to her full six feet and eight inches, I couldn't help but think two things: first, that she was the best argument for drinking milk ever made, and second, that she had some impressive nerve to defy the tacit expectations of Harvard (and of nature) to do what *she* wanted instead. But was she right?

---

*The guy on the rice box doesn't count.

This friction between obligation and desire is universal – just ask Hillary – and will probably never be resolved. Do I do what I am good at? Do I do what I want most? Do I give up retirement and try to become the first female President because I, unlike most, actually could? My constant fear is that I will choose the wrong side; or worse – that I already have.

My ambition comes from knowing that I am capable of achieving great things, and also from taking pride in that fact. On top of feeling an obligation to use the brain I have been given, I also want to prove to myself, the world, the writers of every rejection letter, whomever, that I am neither wasting my talents nor resting on them. Combine that with a few centuries worth of ingrained New England Puritanism, which screams that nothing is of value unless it is difficult, and the result is an ever-climbing standard for "success" that soon resembles a penchant for misery.

> **Masochism – n. 1: pleasure in being abused or dominated; 2: a taste for suffering.**

Despite major guilt, I have somehow managed to let desire do most of the steering in life. In college, I changed my major from Applied Math to English not because I couldn't make it as a cryptographer, but because there were so many books I wanted to read and discuss (and because a life with time for band parties was better than a life crammed full of problem sets). Still, I feel like I gave up somehow. After getting into a few good law schools, I again decided not to go down that road because, while studying law sounded fun, the idea of being a lawyer (and of accumulating more debt) did not appeal to me. Even though I am now blissfully happy as a writer, there is also an overwhelming sense that I have to make up for what I have given up. But what level of literary success is the equivalent of a career as an NSA code breaker, or a White House speech writer, or a public school teacher (like my parents)? This is how ambition becomes self-flagellation.

To satisfy my ambition and assuage my guilt over taking the more enjoyable (and thus, to my conscience, the easier) path in life, I have to achieve something hard. I mean, *really* hard. How else can I explain my ridiculous life choices? I could have taken a traditionally difficult path and become a lawyer, or a teacher, or a scientist, so instead I have chosen not just to write, but to write in the one medium (film) that least values writers, in the one genre (comedy) that gets the least respect, and as a member of the gender (female) that is only grudgingly welcome in the boys' clubhouse. Whose stupid idea was this?

Ambition is great – we should all be striving for something – but the trick, I suppose, is to appreciate the struggle without falling in love with it. When the dream we envision is so ideal as to become nearly impossible, maybe we should start to worry that we're in it more for the pride of survival than for the actual goal. Because if that is the case, then success (should it happen) might ultimately become a disappointment. Be careful what you wish for, as they say.

Or not; I have ranted often about how fairy tales are evil because they teach girls to wait for a perfect partner who doesn't exist, but here I am in my thirties still holding out for a man I can live with. Does that mean I'm sabotaging my happiness, or being patient enough to achieve it? I like to think of myself as an idealist, but as the Democratic Party has demonstrated time and again, "idealist" is just another way of saying "glutton for punishment."

On the other hand, *Fifty Shades of Grey* became a multi-million-dollar property, and a woman my age snagged a ring from George Clooney. Maybe masochism is the way to go after all – if you can survive it.

GEOMETRY

FRACTAL ROCK

Winter is here, I've heard, and we are all now a bunch of snow-flakes.

As a sign-carrying, injustice-protesting, phone-banking, voter-registering, identity-politicking feminist liberal, I am – so the internet tells me – one of the massive snowflakes. Apparently, we are snowflakes either because we are fragile, melt in the face of criticism, and are too frozen inside to know how to take a joke, or because we are each unique, individually beautiful, and en masse able to steamroll hapless victims, shut down roads and highways, and bring all of Westeros to its knees.

Which particular definition of "snowflake" is at any given moment in season seems to be tied directly to how recently the definer has been offended by something, faced opposition to an opinion, or found themselves tweeting up the wrong tree. But whether you're feeling crystalline and ephemeral or ready to wreak the wrath of an ice age, snowflakes are also one thing we can all agree on:

Snowflakes are one of nature's fractals.

Fractals are fascinating, super cool (like snow), and as patterns on paper make for one of the best coloring book themes you could ever hope for. Hours of pure meditative joy – trust me.

They are also one of those things that people have heard of and claim to love but can't actually talk about because they haven't gotten around to taking in the details.*

So, to begin: some basics. While fractals have been around since the existence of snowflakes and nautilus shells and the universe in general, they weren't given a name (by humans) until the mid-1970s. That name comes from the Latin word for broken or fractured ("fractus") because fractals are, in essence, complex and irregular repeating shapes that, when broken into pieces, reveal individual parts that each resemble the original whole. The way each leaf on a fern frond looks like a mini version of the frond itself, or how each floret on a head of broccoli looks like the plant as a whole – that makes them fractals.

Sidebar: I could write an entire thesis about the geometric glory that is a head of Romanesco, with Fibonacci spirals, the golden ratio, and fractal patterns all joyously dancing together in a cruciferous bacchanal of vegetative quantitation. Sure, vegetables are good for your body, but some of them are even better for your mind.

This mini reflection property of fractals is called "self-similarity," which means that each smaller part of itself looks similar to the larger whole. A pure, mathematical fractal – where self-similarity

---

*Like a Ken Burns documentary.

is literally true – can be created by a computer repeating infinite iterations of a simple function in a recursive feedback loop (which means the end result of running the function one time becomes the starting input for the next run, and so on – like you do with priors in Bayesian reasoning). The invention of computers, with their ability to make theoretically infinite processes a reality, allowed fractals to move from an idea based on nature to a functional part of our mathematical language – and also create those aforementioned coloring books I highly recommend you give a try.

But before computers came into play and made fractal geometry a thing, our understanding of it all started with nature's fractals. More specifically, with a man trying to measure the English coastline.

Coastlines are considered fractals because they are generally an irregular, jagged line whose individual segments are each similarly irregular, jagged lines made up of even smaller irregular, jagged parts, and so on and so on until the sea rises up to swallow us all. When the English mathematician Lewis Fry Richardson mused about measuring his country's coastline, it suddenly occurred to him that the answer would depend upon – and change with – whatever he chose to use as a tool. A yard stick would give him one length, but a smaller, more precise tool like a ruler would be able to measure around more of the jagged detail and thus result in a longer distance.

Think of it like measuring a flight of stairs. The easiest way is probably to hold the end of a tape measure at the top edge of the top step, let the tape measure itself slide down the flight of stairs, then ask your gently concussed roommate to read out the result down at the bottom. But if you had to determine the length of a carpet meant to cover that flight of stairs, you would have to take in more detail, measuring the rise and run of each individual step and adding them up, resulting in a much longer distance than your tape measure traveled. The stairs are the same, but suddenly their length is greater. And if next you were to calculate the distance traveled by a tiny bug on those stairs, whose journey involves crawling over each individual fiber of that carpet, the length of the stairs turns out to be even longer.

Suddenly, Lewis Fry Richardson had unleashed the concept of a fourth dimension in geometry – the Fractal Dimension – which adds "complexity" to the already familiar dimensions of length, width, and height. Measure a mountain the traditional way – multiply its height by its width and its length and divide by three – and you get a basic estimate of its volume. Factor the complexity of its rocky, craggy surface into the equation and you get a much more accurate calculation. Mathematicians were understandably excited.

Not only does fractal geometry allow interior designers to take more accurate measurements of Bond villain lairs, Bat Caves, and Fraggle Rock, it also leads to the question of what happens if we keep looking at these complex stairs or coastlines in finer and finer detail? The answer is, they will keep getting longer the more detail we measure.

Fractals demonstrate the paradoxical idea that an infinite distance can be traveled in a finite space. *

Which brings us back to the snowflake, and why it really is the perfect symbol for our modern public discourse. It is *not* because a snowflake melts easily or is collectively capable of violent destruction, but because, as a fractal, the snowflake is a physical manifestation of the fact that while something may at first appear to be a simple speck of frozen water, the closer you look the more its intricate, crystalline complexity starts to appear. And, more often than not, our final determination on an issue depends largely on the way we choose to measure it.

So if, for example, we judge the fates of (mostly) men being exposed in the #MeToo movement by the yardstick of whether they imposed unwanted physical contact on a person, the Harvey Weinsteins and Al Frankens and Joe Bidens all measure up at roughly the same size. When we look closer and apply a bit more sensitive metric, details such as intention and awareness and repentance and change begin to emerge. The closer we look, the more nuance we measure, the more we can factor in the complexity of a person's character and actions to make more thoughtful judgments about what is forgivable, who is capable of redemption, and which Weinstein should be tossed into a lead-lined hole like the toxic garbage that he is.

It's the difference between firing everyone who has ever composed an offensive tweet, or seeing the details of racism, remorse, and Russian troll bots in action.

---

*Again, like a Ken Burns documentary.

Fractals are complex structures made from simple repeated ideas, and fractal geometry is focused on finding order in what appears to be chaotic. We need to inject more of the fractal dimension into our public discourse. Instead of taking the measure of our fellow man with the blunt yardstick of Twitter, we need to use the more nuanced calculations of reputable journalism and, if we can, the most delicate metric of thoughtful, informed conversation.

In the middle of this winter of our discontent, we need to Be the Snowflake. *See* the Snowflake. Embrace the Snowflake in all its infinite fractal complexity. Winter *is here;* do you wanna build a nuanced snowman?

LESSON 16
LOGIC

LOGICAL MYSTERY TOUR

Once upon a short time ago, I spent over twenty minutes arguing with a Time Warner Cable representative about how math works.

My monthly cable bill had suddenly increased by $7 (increased again, I should say, because this was in no way the first time), so I had looked and found a new $7 charge listed for the modem. (The modem I had been using for no charge since…always.) Since no warning had been given for this new charge, I braced myself, cleared my calendar, made sure the food supplies were full and there was something soft nearby for forehead bashing, and called customer service.

The Time Warner representative tried repeatedly to convince me that they had always been charging me $7 for the modem, it was just that now they were listing the fee as its own line item on the bill. I replied that if that were true my bill *total* would not have increased (because, math) but it *had* increased, so there was clearly a new charge for *something*, and would she please just fess up to it already.

After twenty minutes of going 'round and around this point in our own little basic cable version of *Waiting for Godot* ("I recognize that tree!"), she finally succumbed to the power of how numbers work and agreed there was a new fee. I thanked her and agreed to no longer be a Time Warner Cable customer.

While I appreciate that this woman provided the kick I needed to finally bail on cable, our conversation made me – and *still* makes me – want to bang my head against a wall. For nine years, I have spent much of my time helping adults prepare themselves for the rigors of law school, and in that time I have been repeatedly surprised and disheartened – as I was on that phone call – with the general lack of logical reasoning employed by both individual and collective humans.

Logic is important, even if only to save us from Kafkaesque conversations with and murderous fantasies about customer service representatives. If we practiced more logical reasoning in our daily lives, our civilization would be in a much better place.

For one thing, logic allows us to recognize when people (and cable companies, and congressmen) are lying. It does not allow opinions to masquerade as complete arguments, but rather demands factual evidence and actual reasoning be given to support those opinions – including our own. With logic, we can recognize when a statement is technically true ("*Monster Trucks* is the #1 comedy of the year!") but essentially meaningless ("Dude, it's still January") and decide on its significance accordingly. We can also differentiate between a statement of absence ("there is no proof") and one made in the positive ("that proves I didn't do it").

Even more relevant to our current state of debate, practicing logic helps us to stay focused on the actual point at issue, instead of getting distracted by more convenient statements that are off topic. Sure, mental health and how we treat it *is* a major problem in the world, but that isn't a relevant rebuttal to "there should be more gun regulation," any more than "vegans are annoying" addresses whether we should let the pregnant pigs turn around in their crates, or "science is hard" is an argument against global warming. We get better at recognizing when bad-faith arguers try to disprove general trends with a single counterexample, and when other bad-faith arguers try to claim counter-evidence isn't relevant to their point. Practice helps us separate a person's argument from their actual person, but also approach with skepticism an arguer with a track record as a proven liar.

The more we practice logical reasoning, the better we get at recognizing assumptions – including and especially our own – which means we can start distinguishing between the more reasonable assumptions and the ones that make an ass out of u and me. Most importantly, though, the practice of logical reasoning demands that we learn to make and identify valid deductions from the facts at hand. That is what makes logical reasoning so vital to our survival moving forward, because in order to learn to make deductions, we *must* exercise a key skill: creative thinking.

It is no coincidence that Einstein was a skilled violinist while Hitler was a bad painter; creativity and reason go hand in hand. To be deductive is to be able to mentally explore the vast creative possibilities, evaluate them against whatever facts are known, and eliminate them methodically until (if you are lucky) there remains only one. It is to know that there was a mass extinction of dinosaurs, imagine the universe of possible reasons it could have happened, and use the evidence of meteor strikes, the lack of evidence of spontaneous combustion, and miniscule likelihood of alien invasion to conclude that most likely the meteors were the culprit.

(It is also to know that the limited facts demand language like "most likely" instead of "of course it happened that way, how dare you question me?!" or "I don't believe you so no it didn't!")

I know we all think of highly logical people as robots, like Spock, or as actual robots, like Data, but that is only one half of the story. Deductive reasoning requires both methodical *and* *creative* thinking working in tandem, and thus the practice of logical thinking trains us to have flexible minds. But why do we care about having a flexible mind? Because without mental flexibility we can never achieve empathy. Yes, empathy also demands that we have or at least understand human emotions (sorry, Sherlock), but empathy by definition requires the ability to think beyond our own personal experience.

In college, I was once asked by a boy (he was a "boy" in every sense) why I was pro-choice; to answer him, I started by saying, "Well, given my own health issues, I can certainly imagine why someone might need-" and he cut me off by yelling, "It's not about YOU. You're so selfish."

His statement was technically true – it wasn't about me – but meaningless, because it WAS about my ability to put myself in another person's shoes; to imagine circumstances that, while not true for me, may be true for someone in a different place, or time, or dimension of time and space.

A rigid "I would never" is not enough to close the book on any subject. That's great that we would never; it is completely our right to choose to "never" – but somebody would, and shouldn't we at least take the time to listen to, explore, and understand their reasons before we pass judgment?

Without empathy, our social progress – which rests on the evolution of individual minds – could only happen once everyone personally experiences or knows a victim of sexual assault, xenophobia, racial discrimination, homophobia, abuse of power, denial of rights, or just being forced to make a bad choice in a bad situation.

Of course, the sad fact is, most everyone already does. That some people still refuse to acknowledge it defies logic.

LESSON 17
NUMBER THEORY
IRRATIONAL PASTIME

Who's up for some pi?

According to Schoolhouse Rock, three is a magic number – and it is. But just as pi is equal to a little more than three, pi itself is a little more than magical. It is downright metaphorical.

Mathematicians, scientists, and philosophers have been chasing down the elusive number for thousands of years. Pretty much since we gained awareness of numbers themselves, and of round things. It didn't take us long to figure out that the ratio between a circle's circumference and its diameter was a constant number or that the number was just over three, but several hundred lifetimes would pass before we got more accurate than that.

> *What do you get when you divide the circumference of a jack o' lantern by its diameter? Pumpkin pi!*

The true quest for pi was borne out of our desire to "square the circle." In a literal, mathematical sense this means finding a simple – or at least consistent – way to calculate a square with equal area to any given circle. Symbolically, squaring the circle is a much deeper human desire.

Circles have always been symbols of the mysterious. They represent the infinite, even sometimes defined as "a polygon with infinite corners." With no beginning or end point, they symbolize that which is eternal and immeasurable. According to Nietzsche and Matthew McConaughey, time itself is a flat one. Even this essay is circular (it ends where it begins). Circles are unknowable, mesmerizing, spiritual.

Squares, on the other hand, are a symbol of all that is solidly defined. They are firmly knowable, easily measured, comfortably comprehensible. There is a reason one of the earliest words in our culture for the nerdy and rule bound was "square."

To search for an exact value of pi – to seek to square the circle – is to attempt to make the unknowable known. To define the undefined. To contain the infinite. Another term for pi is the "circular constant," or, in other words, a mystery that is rock steady.

What was Sir Isaac Newton's favorite dessert? Apple pi!

Historically, many have considered this quest to understand the mysterious a dangerous game. The poet John Donne wrote the verse, "Eternal God – for whom who ever dare / Seek new expressions, do the circle square, / And thrust into straight corners of poor wit / Thee, who art cornerless and infinite" to explicitly condemn the search for an exact value for pi. Many more, like Archimedes, devoted their entire lives to the quest. All of them died without reaching it.

Because, of course, the quest is impossible. It took us several thousand years, but eventually (by the 18th century) we humans finally proved that the number pi is irrational – its digits go on forever and never repeat. About a hundred years later, we also determined that pi is transcendent, which means it is not the solution to any algebraic equation. Irrational and transcendent – just like the human mind.

Those two vital discoveries – that the circular constant is both never ending or repeating and impossible to equate – combine to prove without doubt that we cannot find a square with equal area to a circle. The circle, quite literally, can never be squared.

> *"Secant, tangent, cosine, sine, 3.14159!"*
> —*MIT cheerleaders*

So the number pi is simultaneously proof that some things can never be known *and* that there are rock-solid constants we can rely on. Constants such as our drive to always dig deeper and know more, even if we can never understand it all. No wonder pi is the most enduringly studied number in human history.

These days, pi continues to symbolically bridge the gap between the mysterious and the defined. It has become our computational bedrock, used to test computers for bugs or weakness, and at the same time our mathematicians are scouring its digits through billions of decimal places (and counting!) in search of any pattern or logic to its order. So far, we've found nothing. It is proving uniquely and stubbornly random.

> *"Knowledge is limited. Imagination circles the world."*
> —*Albert Einstein*

On March 14th, we celebrate this metaphorical number by eating pie, something that is both circular and delicious. We also celebrate another wonder of the universe – Albert Einstein, who was born on 3/14/1879. Einstein himself is a perfect representation of pi's duality, as his life continuously bridged math and creativity, blended science with spirituality, and mixed social consciousness with humor. He understood better than nearly anyone the perfect paradox embodied by pi: that the more we learn, the less we know.

Or, to put it in terms of the constant itself, the wider the circle of light, the larger the circumference of darkness. (Not an Einstein quote, but one of *his* favorite sayings.)

Thanks for the reminder, Albert. And…

Who's up for some pi?

A PORTRAIT OF THE ARTIST AS A GROWN-ASS WOMAN

Once upon a time, and a very good time it was, there was a dream. There was inspiration and motivation and daring and excitement. She was going to conquer the world and with a voice in her ear and endless story in her heart she knew that she could.

* * *

The land of creation is populated by liars. Its waters look deep but when stepped in are shallow, and the language is not how it sounds.

—How is it yes means maybe and maybe means don't hold your breath? She never could understand or remember. She never learned to speak WhatsInItForMe.

But there are sparkly people, too, and she loves them! There are brilliant ideas and shiny talents; there is work and play and work and collaboration. O the collaboration! Yes, she says, and yes again. Let's do something, or another thing, or lunch. A new project, new spark, new yes and yes I will Yes.

* * *

How can a world so small and crowded feel so empty sometimes? She has uncovered the challenge of living in the world while working in her head.

—It's far better than the reverse, she reminds herself.

She watches friends change and fade and move on to better things, to better people. One by one some give up. She dreads the day she is faced with the same decision, wondering how one could possibly stop.

—Better odds for the rest of us. She secretly loves the acquired wisdom such ugly understanding betrays.

* * *

—This work is fantastic! Can you make it less smart?

—I love everything about this. Can you make it about a man?

—A brilliant new voice! Can you take out everything that makes it different?

Some create while others calculate, she learns. She wishes the calculators had as much faith in humanity as she does.

Stupidity and fear increase with power. With each comment she learns to find the useful in the self-indulgent slop. She realizes she has a choice. Not every suggestion has to matter. Even if it's right, she decides if it is right for her. She learns to listen to herself.

* * *

Success is a carrot dangling, tantalizing up ahead. There is work, and money, but never the meal. She drags the weight of experience one step closer and grasps; victory keeps pace. One more step, one more reach, one more miss. With each try the weight gets heavier. Her legs get stronger. The distance gets smaller. But there is still distance.

She played Lucy once in *You're a Good Man, Charlie Brown*. It sucks to be on the other side of the football.

* * *

—Why can't my work speak for itself? Why do I have to learn to market to people?

—If only it worked that way. This is a business too, she explains. People have to see the dollar signs.

Mentoring reminds her how much she knows after all the years, how much she has to offer. It is good to give back, help, feel useful. She hopes they won't look too closely and see she's a fraud.

—What is the best strategy for breaking in?

—When you find out you can tell the rest of us.

She explains time and again there is no best way. Everyone has a different story. Everyone has the same answer: whatever works. Time and again she watches their faces fall to frustration. She remembers the feeling. It doesn't get better, she wants to tell them. Unless it does and she just doesn't know it yet.

—It really is true that if anything else can make you happy, you should do it.

—They tell the same thing to the clergy, her student replies.

—Sometimes it's hard to tell them apart.

Isolation, devotion, a calling. The joke works because it's true. She wonders if she accidentally took a vow of celibacy at some point.

* * *

Night is dark, but feels darker. The city moves constantly, yet nothing changes. She wants desperately to give up. What if the years ahead look just like the ones stretched behind?

Stopping would be easy, logistically – she could teach, go back to school. Stopping spiritually is impossible. The voice is there. She has something to say and the ability to say it. Her drive to be heard will never fade; stopping just means desire with no hope.

But she lacks means. Substance and skill are useless without means. It feels like the means will never come.

Death would stop desire. She briefly considers it; the moment is one moment too scary. Her practical side objects: too much willpower, love, guilt. She wishes there were better reasons to get out of bed.

> —OOF. Okay, I'll feed you! Now please get your fuzzy butt off my bladder.

She is reminded why she adopted the cat in the first place. Who rescued whom, really?

* * *

Nov. 9: Another birthday without the gift of work from anyone supposedly invested in my career. Another *day* is frustrating enough. If I make it to 40 in the same situation, it may kill me. Although I'm pretty sure I said that about 37. And 35. Time for champagne!

Nov. 26: Today I get to be with family. As rough as the last 13 years have been, at least I haven't had to deal with parental disappointment or a lack of love. I give thanks for family.

Dec. 1: It's tempting to hate the agent who refuses to sign female comedy writers, but he's not wrong. The odds are for-*never* in our favor re: work. But my motivation is starting to return. Spirits are up.

Dec. 27: Winter is coming? I'm pretty sure it's here. A *Game of Thrones* marathon can ease me through the end of the year, but I need preparation to survive. New projects; new strategies; new sparks. Time to work.

Jan. 1: Welcome, O life! I go to encounter for the millionth time the reality of experience and to forge in the smithy of my soul the uncreated story of my future. Stand me now and ever in good stead.

Los Angeles 2016

My thanks to James Joyce for writing something I struggled with the first time, started to understand the second time, and have loved every single time since.

MYTHOLOGY

ROCK, PAPER, SISYPHUS, SHOOT ME

I imagine if Sisyphus were alive today he would be a New Hampshire-ite, like me. (A New Hampshirino?) He would at least be a New Englander. Heck, he may already *be* Bernie Sanders. And I don't just say this because of the futility that is shoveling a plowed-in driveway in the midst of a New England winter.

Everyone thinks of endless futility when Sisyphus is invoked, but rarely do we remember *why* he was sentenced to such a fate. In his life before metaphor, King Sisyphus was a practical leader who placed his own judgment and passions above silly customs and superstitions like "the gods." He also made the most of every moment he faced.

Zeus steals the river god's daughter for his own version of Fifty Shades of a Rape Fantasy and no one dares to speak up? Not Sisyphus – he's all, "I'll tell you where your daughter is, river god, if you promise to give my people water." That's good leadership. Angry Zeus sends Death to chain Sisyphus up in punishment? Clever boy says, "Hey, Death, you mind showing me how those chains work first, so I'm less nervous?" BAM. Death in chains, King S back on Earth – Live Free or Die, baby. Literally.

Even when he eventually *did* die, Sisyphus refused to stop living. He talked Persephone into letting him back up amongst the living, "Just to haunt the wife a little," then simply refused to leave until he'd had his fun. Sure, his lust for life and complete disregard for what is "supposed to" happen made his ultimate torment by the ethereal authorities inevitable, but I'm pretty sure Sisyphus would have done it all anyway. You only live twice; what is an eternity of monotonous labor in exchange for greatness?

Great victories are always balanced by great struggle some-how, whether it be before or after they arrive.* Call it Newton's Third Law of Emotion: for every high, there's a low. The problem is that in the midst of the struggle, in those darkest moments – as our strength is on the verge of giving out – it is impossible to know if we are about to be victorious over Death or about to watch that damn rock roll back down the hill for the umpteenth time as punishment for some good we've already enjoyed.

There is a moment near the end of the book *The Two Towers* that is one of my favorites because it perfectly captures this uncertainty. Frodo, after months of mental torment and in the middle of a seemingly endless upward climb into Mordor, is feeling understandably desperate. To distract his friend from complete surrender, the stalwart Samwise starts talking about adventures:

---

*(My sister-in-law believes this is especially true with regards to pregnancy vs. childbirth vs. the resulting children, and from my limited observations so far, I'm convinced she's right).

"I used to think that they were things the wonderful folk of the stories went out and looked for... But that's not the way of it with the tales that really mattered... Folk seem to have been just landed in them... But I expect they had lots of chances, like us, of turning back, only they didn't. And if they had, we shouldn't know, because they'd have been forgotten. We hear about those as just went on – and not all to a good end."

Sam then asks the magic question: "I wonder what sort of tale we've fallen into?"

"I wonder," says Frodo, "but I don't know. And that's the way of a real tale...the people in it don't know. And you don't want them to."

Frodo is convinced at this point that he is pushing a ring up a hill in complete futility, but of course *we* know (spoiler alert) that he will end up victorious over death. I like to re-read this part of Tolkien's masterpiece in the midst of my darker moments. True, Frodo is attempting to destroy the source of pure evil for the survival of all living things and I am merely trying to bring some respectful and multi-dimensional portrayals of women to our modern mythology, but a struggle doesn't have to be epic to completely suck sometimes.

Hollywood may not be Mordor, but it sure can come close. The need to write is my ring/rock, and the patriarchal, nepotistic power structure is my uphill battle. But frankly, everyone has their version of the Sisyphean struggle at some point in life – especially if you have the nerve to pursue a dream.

Over the years, I have felt far more like Sisyphus on the hill than Frodo in the midst of a dark tunnel leading eventually to light, but like Frodo I know that my feelings are no indicator of the ultimate outcome. If we strivers are lucky, in these darkest times we find ourselves in the company of a Samwise Gamgee – someone to give a little perspective, or at the very least a distraction for a moment or two.

I have been thus blessed in the form of a practical and wise best friend who, over the course of our thirty-year journey, has saved my soul from despair more times than there are hills to climb. Because of her (and a heroically supportive family) I am prepared to keep pushing my rock no matter how many times it rolls back down the hill.

Life could always be worse, after all. As my own Samwise put it once, "Sisyphus is still better than syphilis!" Truer words have never been spoken.

Full-Frontal Nerdity 104: Life (Coping)

LESSON 20
QUANTUM MECHANICS

QUANTUM CRASHING (OR, CRISIS ON INFINITE ME)

I once spent a half-decade worth of March 1sts marking the anniversary of the best thing that had ever happened to me that hadn't actually happened yet. I know, it sounds like science fiction (*What?! How could it have happened and not happened at the same time? Are you Gwyneth Paltrow in Sliding Doors?* No, because I loathe Coldplay with every ounce of my soul.), but really it is just the unfortunate, discombobulating nature of the film industry – and any other industry that mixes artistry and business. Things happen, but then they aren't "official" until many various other things happen, and because those various other things could possibly not ever happen, no one in the know is allowed to talk about anything they know about in terms of specifics, even though they want to shout their rare success from the rooftops.

Needless to say, it creates a great deal of Trouble when you're running around with A Head Full of Dreams but the Gravity of what's at stake is holding you down, and you're feeling like The World Turned Upside Down, but only time can Fix You. (I really need to stop listening to Top 40 radio – there is inexplicably way too much Chris Martin for anyone's good.) For five whole years, I lived in Hollywood Limbo, celebrating something I could not celebrate, having accomplished something I had not technically accomplished. (Spoiler: in the end it never happened.)

Basically, I spent five years stuck between parallel universes: one in which I was a *working* professional writer with a movie deal and a credit and many other traditional markers of success, and another in which I was a professional writer who so far had nothing tangible to show for it. I was Schrödinger's cat, stuck in a lead box with a possibly-decaying radioactive particle, both alive and dead at the same time, desperate for someone to open the lid and define me one way or the other.*

On the plus side, I now know what it feels like to operate on a quantum level. On the down side, it sucked big time and I was relieved when it ended.

The most common theory of parallel universes – the Many Worlds Interpretation – springs from the theory of quantum mechanics. As I mentioned in *Quantum Leaping*, quantum particles don't exist in just one state or another (moving or still, for example), but in what Neils Bohr called a "superposition": they exist in all possible states at the same time. Bohr noted that our

---

*Okay, I very much wanted to be defined in the way that involved loads of money.

observation of them is what breaks superposition and forces them to, basically, pick a state and stick with it. (A concept Schrodinger demonstrated his deep frustration with by sticking a poor hypothetical cat in a box with hypothetical poison.)

In the middle of my less-than-super superposition, I *desperately* wanted someone to try to observe my career so it would be forced to pick a reality. Of course, it could (and ultimately did) pick the dead cat reality instead of the live one, so I also desperately wanted to stay in the box for as long as possible, and there you have the perfect metaphor for the nauseating terror that is being suddenly face-to-face with everything you've ever wished for.

The many worlds theory of parallel universes goes one step beyond Bohr and says that while *to us* an observed particle looks like it chose just one of its possible states, it *actually* split the universe into several realities – one for each of its possible states. So, when we open the box to check on the cat, in *our* world she leaps out alive and pissed off, but we also create a parallel universe in which Fluffy was not so lucky.

And thus it goes, on and on, splitting off parallel realities with each point of decision or action. Fluffy jumps out of the box and can either scratch our face off or hide under the bed; boom: two more worlds exist, one with eyes glaring out from the darkness and one where we're bleeding profusely. We, of course, see only one continuous reality from our perspective, but just on the other side of the fabric of space-time there are other versions of us with more or less blood on our faces and/ or a dead cat.

I find the idea of a multiverse comforting at times like those anniversaries, not just because it nicely captures the schizophrenic feeling that comes from being both victorious and braced for failure at the same time, but also because it helps put things in perspective. Naturally, it was extremely difficult to be on the verge of a dream come true for so long, and to watch that dream be deferred again and again until it ultimately died. I felt like Archie 'Moonlight' Graham from *Field of Dreams,* standing on the base line of a magical baseball diamond, one step away from the life I was meant to live, but for five whole years instead of five seconds. Medicine was Archie Graham's true calling so he stepped over that baseline, and I also wanted to step into my life-long career. But with each day that I waited, I became increasingly terrified that writing would turn out to be my version of Moonlight's baseball career – something I came so close to, had within my grasp, but never quite caught.

And on top of that, I was mortified that in my thirties I was still occasionally barely able to pay rent.

It is nearly impossible in times like that, when we feel helpless and on the verge of hopeless, not to examine the path that led up to that point and our many choices along the way. The "How did I get here?" "What if I'd done *this* instead?" mental spinning that is not good for anyone. To stop myself, I instead like to think about the fact that somewhere, out in the multiverse, there exist theoretical versions of me that *did* make different choices – many of them worse ones – and that no matter how frustrating, depressing, embarrassing, or just plain crappy I consider my life and myself right in that moment, somewhere there is a parallel universe with a version that is worse. Somewhere out there, there is even *the worst* version of me that could possibly be. Suddenly, things don't seem all that bad.

Of course, there also exists the infinitesimal possibility that *I am* that worse possible version of me. Crap. Does anyone have a radioactive particle and a lead box I can crawl into?

Elizabethan Drama

Instagramlet (Get Thee to Unpluggery)

To tweet, or not to tweet – that is the question;
Whether 'tis nobler off the line to suffer
The stings and harrows of outrageous comments,
Or to type reams against a sea of trollers
And by opposing end them. To like, retweet –
No more; and by delete to say we end
The headache and the thousand cyber shocks
The web is host to. 'Tis a disconnection
Desperately to be wished. To post, to tweet –
To tweet, perchance to SCREAM. Ay, there's the rub.
For in that tweet of wrath, what screams may come
When we have rattled off our mental bile,
Must give us pause. There's the Reply
That makes calamity of logged-in life.

For who would bear the links and shames online,
Th'obsessives wrong, the proud men's buffon'ry,
The pangs of tagged old loves, the trolls irate,
The insolence of bot-heads, and the spurns
Of posts that merit few if any Likes…
When he himself might peace and quiet make
With a broke modem? Who would Facebook bear –

To gloss and status-hype a weary life –
But for the dread of what is off the net:

The un-updated country, from whose road
No traveler checks in or 'Grams their meal,
And makes us rather live those lives we have
Than share with followers we know not of?
Thus, consciousness makes cowards of us all,
And thus the natural glue of real connection
Is cybered o'er with hash-tagged bytes of thought,
And intercourses of points rich and cogent
Eggplant and poop emojis turn awry
And lose their satisfaction.

LESSON 22
STATISTICS

I WAS TOLD THERE WOULD BE NO MATH AT THIS DEBATE

Odds are, someone at some point has quoted Einstein's definition of insanity to you: "Doing the same thing over and over again and expecting different results." I love this quote for several reasons, the top two being that there is no evidence Einstein ever said it, and it is not what insanity actually is. Yet somehow, by people saying it over and over in hope that it is true, it has become true in our conventional wisdom. Isn't that the kind of paradox that is supposed to rip a hole in space-time and make the universe eat itself?

The dictionary definition of insanity is being deranged or unsound of mind enough to be divorced from reality and thus responsibility. Which nicely demonstrates the root of many problems with our current public discourse – it is Einstein Nutters versus Webster Loons.

Someone needs to impose some Nurse Ratched-level tough love on the world, so here I am, with math.

Back in chapter one, I applied Bayesian reasoning (probabilistic thinking) to relationships, in order to get a better understanding of how illogical we often are in matters of the heart. It was fun! And I started to notice something quite interesting about the math, something that has been increasingly relevant as the clash between Science and Faith in our culture has escalated.

To recap: Bayesian reasoning is a process that involves estimating the likelihood of things, then reassessing that likelihood with each new piece of information. In short – and I know this is a dirty word – Bayesian thinkers *evolve* their ideas over time, getting ever closer to understanding.

If this sounds familiar, it is because probabilistic thinking is how we learn. *Hey, that thing on the stove is shiny and pretty – I bet it will feel good too. Ouch. Nope. That did not feel pretty. Maybe pretty things don't always feel good. Hey, that tiger over there is really beautiful. Maybe this time...* and so on. Eventually, we get a feel for the odds.*

The formula representing this process – Bayes's Theorem – is simply a mathematical expression of logic at work. It centers on three variables: our original level of certainty about something (x), the likelihood of whatever new piece of info we have if that something is true (y), and the likelihood of the new piece of info if that something is not true (z). That's it!

When we reassess in the face of a new piece of information, we simply multiply our original level of certainty by the probability

---

*Or die.

that our theory is still true (xy), then divide that by all possibilities – our original certainty (x) times the probability it's still true (y) PLUS our original *uncertainty* (1-x) times the probability of the theory being *false given our new info* (z). In math, that reads:

$$\frac{XY}{(XY)+(1-X)Z}$$

That's the most advanced it gets, I promise. What I started to find interesting as I played around with the math is how the impact of new information changes the more confident we are at the outset. Let me demonstrate with an example involving something totally uncontroversial: birth control.

Take two people, one who is super confident that I am a good little girl who keeps her knees closed (we'll call him "My Dad"), and another who is willing to bet the farm that I am a total slut (we'll call him "Rush Limbaugh"). They are both men, because involving a woman in a conversation about birth control would be ridiculous. Now, what happens to their respective outlooks when we introduce a new piece of information into their worlds: the fact that I use birth control?

My Dad starts out with only 10% concern that I am a Promiscuous Girl (x = .1), while Rush is 90% sure I am sex crazed, since I am unmarried (x = .9). Variable y is the probability that I would use birth control if I *am indeed* a floozy, which is clearly about 95% – what floozy worth her salt wouldn't use birth control? Variable z is the probability that I would use it if I am *not* handing out my free milk all over town. Since all women are either virgins or whores, that's clearly 5%.

When we plug those probabilities into the formula, we see that My Dad, who is faced with new information that is contradictory to his original belief, skyrockets to a new 68% certainty that I am a Daughter of Questionable Morals. As for Rush, whose original outlook is being confirmed by the new information, he goes from 90% sure to 99% sure I am a good time to call. Had we presented both of them with opposite information – like a purity ring on my finger – My Dad's fears of parental failure would have dropped from 10% to .6%, and Rush would suddenly have to grapple with a mere 32% chance of my nymphomania.

Of course, my probabilities here are extreme, but the formula holds: the more confident we are in a theory at the outset, the more devastating contrary information becomes. As it should be! If we truly think an outcome is "inconceivable" and then it happens, we either have to admit that there is a very good chance we're wrong or accept that the word "inconceivable" does not mean what we think it means. Remember that the next time you are baffled by the level of denial a person will cling to in the face of facts that contradict their beliefs. Especially remember it when the person clinging desperately (and sometimes expletively) to denial might be you.

But in addition to demonstrating the shock that can come from discovering we might be wrong, a funny thing happens to the formula when extreme confidence turns the corner into absolute certainty: new information suddenly loses all impact. When $x = 1$ (we are 100% sure of something), the formula reduces to $y/(y + 0z)$, which equals 1 no matter what y and z

are. When x = 0 ("Inconceivable!"), the fraction becomes 0/(0 + z), which is always zero.

In other words, there is no amount of evidence, experience, or new information that will change the mind of someone who has absolute certainty they are right. Proving once and for all with math that there is no arguing with believers.*

If you got this far, you are probably tired, because math is hard. Not in the sense that it requires a Y-chromosome (I'm looking at you, Larry Summers), but in the sense of hard work. Math is work; logic is work; being open minded requires the effort of reassessment. Faith, on the other hand, is easy. Not real faith, as defined in the dictionary ("belief in something for which there is no proof"), but the Faith demonstrated too often these days: belief despite all evidence of any kind – including direct evidence to the contrary.

You want the kicker? Thomas Bayes, from whom Bayesian reasoning gets its name, was an 18th-Century minister. Put that in your censer and smoke it.

I think it's time for the universe to eat itself now.

---

*Or Beliebers – ugh.

ONCE UPON A TIME WARP – A BRIEF HISTORY OF LEAP DAY

It's a tale quite literally as old as time: one of the greatest innovations of human timekeeping in history is credited to "Father of Leap Day" Julius Caesar, and where did he get the idea? From a woman, of course.

Gather round, kids, for a brief story:

Once upon a time, there was a Prince with a Problem. His people, the Romans, were having some trouble keeping track of things. They, like most of humanity, had adopted a lunar calendar – first with only ten months (because, in a move that would make George R.R. Martin proud, winter was a "monthless time"), then eventually with January and February added to bring it to twelve. But if the Prince and his countrymen had bothered to ask, any woman could have told them that letting your life be ruled by a lunar cycle is just asking for trouble. And it was!

The Prince's trouble was that the Man on the Moon takes on average 29.5 days to complete one of his cycles, which adds up to a 354-day year after twelve. Mother Earth, on the other hand, has more to do (someone has to keep the house tidy); she takes roughly 365.25 days to get all the way around the sun, which made the Roman calendar a full 11.25 days too short. Bummer. In just a few years, this communication gap had wreaked complete havoc, landing the Ides of March on the Ides of April, and that just sounds silly.

Like the Classic men that they were, the Prince and his Romans chose to simply ignore this inconvenient problem until it got so big that they finally couldn't; then they "fixed" it by inserting a random extra month into the year now and then, forcing that rascal Spring back where she was supposed to be.

Effective? Yes. Functional? Maybe. But much like a frat house, this was no way to live.

In a different part of the world, a Queen named Cleopatra and her Egyptians had been listening to the Earth Mother and thus had devised a brilliant strategy for living in harmony with Nature. They kept a calendar of twelve tidy 30-day months, then made up the excess time with a five-day party at the end of each year. Every fourth year, that party went for six days.

Kids, if this sounds like the best idea humankind has ever had, you are right. Modern comforts may be nice, but we really missed the boat on that one.

By the time Julius Caesar met Cleopatra, things had gotten way out of hand for the Romans. I mean, seriously out of hand – they'd ignored their time problem so long that Spring was hiding in Summer and snow was falling in May. Julius was impressed by Cleopatra's brilliant calendar (and by everything else about her because she was amazing), so he did what usually happens in these situations: he stole her idea, made it a little less good, and proudly declared it to be his own. Typical.

First, Julius had to get his Roman calendar back on track, which could have happened by letting time take its course, but was more fun to do with brute force. (Brutus force? That would come later.) Declaring 46 B.C. the "Year of Confusion" (no kidding – that's real) Julius Caesar made it 445 days long and forced that sneaky Spring Equinox back to late March, where it belonged. He then scrapped Cleo's New Year's Epic Eve idea and instead sprinkled those extra days around the calendar (making his own month the biggest, *of course*), and decreed that every fourth year one extra day would be added to the end – which, for the Romans, was February.

Way to kill the week-long party, Julius. Way to kill the party.

And everyone lived happily ever after in harmony with Nature – except that they didn't. There was a dark storm brewing, and it was called Accuracy. You see, kids, the problem is that Mother Earth only takes *roughly* 365.25 days to circle the sun. She *actually* takes 365.2422 days, which means that adding a full day to every fourth year (a full quarter for each year) then made the Roman calendar on average 11.2 minutes too LONG.

This seems like a small problem, sure, but like grains of sand in an hour glass, after a while it adds up. In 128 years, the whole calendar was off by a full day, and by the time of Pope Gregory XIII more than 1500 years later, that sneaky bugger Spring was back in April instead of March. Once again, the man in charge took drastic measures, removing ten days from October 1582 (no Halloween candy for you, kids), and declaring that, going forward, every century year – 1600, 1700, etc. – would have no Leap Day, unless that year was also divisible by 4.

That's right, kids; bet you didn't know how special that Leap Day was in 2000.

And so, with this new "Gregorian" calendar (because *of course* he renamed it after himself), we've got the whole 365.2422 days per year problem sorted out. For a while, anyway. It's still not perfect, but it will be 3,300 years before we're off by a whole day again. Let those guys worry about it.

The End*

*Or is it? The buried feminist roots of Leap Day seem to have caused some residual guilt that has seeped out in the form of misguided attempts at female empowerment. In Ireland and the U.K., Leap Day became traditionally the one day women were allowed to propose to men – and had to be compensated (with money or clothes) if turned down. Sure, it's a totally sexist idea, but at least it gave us a cute Amy Adams rom com. In the U.S., this tradition became "Sadie Hawkins Day" (celebrated November 15th in common (i.e. non-leap) years), and in one city –

Aurora, IL – single women are deputized on Leap Day to arrest single men. Man, that's a version of Wayne's World I would love to write someday.

But I say that we take this cautionary tale of losing Cleopatra's genius to the less-competent maneuverings of arbitrarily powerful men and instead learn the obvious lesson it has to teach us: we should always listen to black women in the first place. If we had in leap year 2016, perhaps President Hillary would have reinstated that week-long New Year's party by now.

LESSON 24
GENDER STUDIES
THE XX FACTOR

My first official writing job on a TV series was brought to me by the letter X. Specifically, the letter X without the letter Y.

After a friend of mine from my improv days sold a pilot script, he and his writing partner were tasked with putting together a six-man staff to complete a six-episode season. They took those instructions literally, promptly hiring four male friends to join them.

A little later, my buddy randomly spotted me in a hallway after a comedy show and this is how it went down: "Oh, hey!" (Me: Hey.) "I'm writing a series." (Me: Congratulations!) "We staffed the show already," (Me: Awesome for you.) "but we're thinking maybe we should have a girl in the room too, for the perspective. You're the only girl I know who writes." (Me in my head: This is not true. I know your friends.) "Send me a sample?" (Me: No problem.) I sent him two screenplays and was immediately hired.

As origin stories go, it makes for a pretty lame graphic novel, but I still like to tell it. Because most people miss the point entirely.

Male writers tend to zero in on the double gender standard, while simultaneously demonstrating impressive ignorance; "You only got the job because you're a woman! You're so lucky to have a guaranteed spot at the table."

Um, NO. I got the job the same proud way my four male colleagues got it: nepotism. But I was the *only* staffer with *any* professional screenwriting experience, and yet I was still hired last, as an afterthought, to fill a gender quota. True, my lack of a Y-chromosome was the difference between being hired last and not being hired at all, but if I *had* the Y-chromosome I would have been hired first without question – or probably been hiring my own staff for my own show. Hiring me to be "the girl in the room" didn't end sexism any more than electing Barack Obama ended racism.

Most other people take an optimistic view of the story; "Isn't it great your friend was wise enough to recognize the value of a female voice? We should celebrate him as a shining example of enlightenment and inclusive hiring!"

Again, NO. I don't believe in showering praise on people who "choose" to accept well-established information. Like Kindergarten graduations and participation trophies, it rewards people for doing something that should have been automatic anyway. You acknowledge the universe is billions of years old? Yes, yes, you're very smart. Now shut up. Science, history, anecdotal evidence, and the fluctuating quality of Saturday Night Live have all proven time and again that any collaborative endeavor is improved when there is an even mix of male and female voices involved. (Notice I said *a mix* – I may play host to a couple of confused cats, but neither they nor I are against feminism, because we are all well aware that equality is its true goal.) Yes, my friend was right to want "a girl in the room", but this epiphany didn't make him anything more than the kid who shows up to all the little league games but picks dandelions in the outfield. Hardly an MVP.

So what is the point of my origin story? It's that The Most Interesting Man in the World is the devil.

They say the greatest trick the devil ever pulled was convincing the world he doesn't exist. While I find that statement confusing given the number of people I see on the news screaming about other people burning in hell, the sentiment applies pretty well to sexism. The true tragedy of how I got my first TV job is the part nobody – including me – noticed.

In the heated 2008 battleground that was the Democratic Presidential primary, there was a lot of debate about which candidate had it worse – the one facing racism or the one facing sexism. While both legacies are uniquely horrible, and everyone loses the Oppression Olympics (so we should never try to compete), that primary began to make clear one particularly devilish fact about sexism – a fact that was brutally and glaringly confirmed eight years later in the 2016 race: far too many women buy into the foundational belief that their genetics somehow make them inferior or less worthy. It's hard enough to battle the devil you know is standing right in front of you; sexism is too often the devil we don't.

Women commit as many, if not more, sexist acts against women than the men of this world, and we do it far too often to ourselves without even noticing. We judge each other, demand perfection from each other, blame each other, and fear the implications of each other's success on our own choices. Too often we buy into the idea that there are legitimate grounds for having different expectations, standards, and rules for ourselves than those for men.

The real point of my origin story is that, despite my ability to recognize my friend's gender stupidity and roll my eyes at *how* I got the job from him, I remained completely oblivious to my own bias against myself. I walked into that writers' room on day one *not* confident because I knew I was the only staffed writer with experience, *not* comfortable because I already knew three of the six men and had performed comedy with them as an equal, but *instead* thinking, "I hope I can keep up. I hope they think I'm funny. I hope I manage to pull my weight."

I had more experience and skill than any of my male coun-terparts (I was ultimately the only writer who maintained her credit or was kept on for more work); I had an Ivy League education and a well-honed comedic voice; I had a solid self-respect and an enviable work ethic – both resulting from a lifetime of guidance by ideal parental role models; I was loved and loving, praised and proud, supported and strong. In short: I had the benefit of every possible privilege short of wealth and a penis when I walked into that writers' room, with great hair and a cherry outfit on top.

If *even I* walked in assuming I was the weakest link, what chance does any girl have?

LESSON 25
EASTERN PHILOSOPHY

ZEN AND THE ART OF YOGA CYCLE

Breathe in....
Breathe out...
Breathe in...
Fall over.

If you ever spend more than about 30 minutes in Los Angeles, someone will almost surely talk to you about the life-altering qualities of yoga. Most likely this person will also casually drop some Sanskrit, humblebrag about their most recent "struggle" to master some pose that involves a foot behind their head, and possibly even whip off a handstand right in front of you for good measure.

Despite all their peacocking (also known as *mayaurasana*), these yogis are not wrong; whether it leads to improvement or permanent damage of some kind, practicing yoga *will* impact your life.

There are many potential benefits to yoga, and people come to it for myriad reasons: stress relief, injury repair, strength building, improved flexibility, peer pressure, cool party tricks… (I can drink in tree pose…in heels!) Even though I personally started yoga to combat my duel devils of sciatica and road rage, no doubt the best thing I get out of the practice is humility. With occasional face-planting humiliation.

It is important to practice humility, and doubly so if nature has blessed you with any particular gift. Be it talent, charisma, intellect, or perfect teeth, those born with advantage need to be reminded of our limits. That was my favorite (and least favorite) thing about being at Harvard – the reminder, at almost every turn, that no matter how good I got at something there was most certainly someone better. Knowing that keeps you motivated, for one thing, and more importantly keeps your ego in check.

Yoga can provide the same service, without the six-figure tuition.* There will always be something in a yoga class to keep you humble, whether it be the balance part, the flexibility part, the strength part, or the meditation. For every day that you manage to pull off a levitating arm balance or transition into a Jedi-level inversion, there will also be a day when you can barely fold forward without falling on your face. Because that's life. Some days are full of pic-a-nic baskets, and others smack yogi with a booboo.

---

*Though if you really want to pay that much, I'm sure there is a studio in Bel Air somewhere that will accommodate.

A friend of mine, with whom I share the typically hyperactive mind of most nerdy people, once joined me in a lament about the tumultuous highs and lows of our yoga practice. She doesn't mind the more embarrassing physical flops all that much – heck, she sometimes seeks them out by attempting aerial yoga – but she instead dreads her inevitable inability to sustain any held poses with grace or anything resembling mental focus. In the yoga sutras, Concentration is job one – necessary before we can hope to either Practice or Progress to spiritual Liberation – so it is a major element of any good yoga class. Concentration begins with the simple act of attention, more specifically being able to keep your attention on the moment at hand, instead of being distracted by every tickle and itch, that wonderful smell you've discovered, and all of the glorious humanity on display around the room (this is especially hard in naked yoga classes). This particular friend of mine happens to be the single most observant person I know, so I understand her difficulty in focusing inward when surrounded by so much external stimulation and comedic potential. (I also *love* her resulting yoga stories.)

Her struggle with focus is one I can certainly relate to, but it is also what draws me particularly to the types of yoga classes that feature extended holds. I like a challenge. While I am not all that externally observant in class – both because of my nature and because I remove my glasses, reducing the world to a pleasant, colorful blur – I do have a major tendency to live in my head. Most pose-holding down time, which is supposed to be about experiencing the moment, turns quickly into my brain reminding me what I forgot to put on my grocery list, immediately thinking of the perfect line of dialogue which I currently have no ability to write down, and suddenly playing the theme song from *Flashdance* on a loop inside my head.

Plus, there is also the fact that yoga is a physical activity, which means more often than not the pose you are trying to sustain requires effort from some reluctant muscle or stretches some tendon that is simply not having it that day. The brain tends to get distracted by those nagging parts, too.

To combat my own wandering mind and make at least some attempt at concentration, I rely first on the thing they tell everyone to focus in on in yoga: breathing. And this is *great* if you can sustain it. When you reach that point where your body is loudly and clearly *not having any more of this nonsense* (and let's face it, some days that is about three seconds in), you only have a few options. One is to bail out into a resting pose, the three most common being child's pose (*balasana*) corpse pose (*shavasana*), and happy baby pose (*ananda balasana*); from their names you can tell that they are each about as productive a position for exercise as they are for a productive life. You could do the opposite of bailing, which is to do nothing except continue to whine, curse, and scream bloody murder inside your head for the duration, and how's that strategy been working out for you so far? Or, hear me out, you can find a way to deal with it. Breathing really is the best way to deal with whatever "it" may be. Focusing on the ins and outs of air flow immediately pushes the less-helpful thoughts out of the mind, keeps us living in the moment which ultimately makes time pass much faster, and remarkably proves time and again that a forgotten irritation is an irritation that is as good as gone.

Unfortunately, it is not always so easy to be all about that breath. Eventually…the compulsions kick in. Breathing in and out turns into breathing evenly in and out, which means counting the beats as you breathe, which soon becomes more counting than breathing, and eventually mostly counting, and that means we're back on the passage of time, and suddenly you're right back where you started, with quadriceps screaming, and an itch on your nose, and *when is this going to be over already you monste*—Aaaaand….

Breathe in….

Breathe out…

Regroup.

So that's when you need a plan B. On days when my mind is particularly active or distracted or both, I turn my weakness into strength and wrangle that mental energy into what I call my "yoga cycle." I can't stop my attention from jumping from one thing to the next, but I can direct it to jump with purpose. It becomes an active mental inventory, focused on the task at hand, done in rhythm with my breathing. *Foot position okay? Great. Knee pointed out over the toe? Fixed it. Core engaged, pelvis tilted right? Got it. How clenched is my jaw?* …and so on and so on and so on until I've checked in with every piece of my body, from pinkie to brain. And when I get to the bottom I go back to the top of the slide…

There are several reasons I love this process, the first being that it works. My mind stays focused on something relevant, I stay in the pose, and neither of us breaks out singing Irene Cara chart toppers.

Second, it consistently reminds me of a valuable lesson about multi-tasking – specifically that multi-tasking is a load of hooey. It may *seem* like I'm keeping all the plates spinning as I think about each of my various parts in succession, but *really* the process becomes an endless cycle of: *Hey, when did my foot get crooked? Knee – I thought I told you to be pointed over* there. *Who okayed that bend in my lower back? And when the heck did my core decide to relax? And why is my stupid jaw always so clenched?!* And so on and so on… There is no such thing as actually giving your attention to two things at once. (It's why the breathing works as a distraction.) You are either focused on one thing or focused on nothing. The trick is giving your attention to each of the one things you care about in a balanced order that works.

Finally, the reason I love the mental yoga cycle – and the reason I love yoga in general – is that each time I visit a body part I am forced to accept my imperfection. No matter how many times I work my brain around my body, there will always be something out of line. Always some part slacking off. There will always be some ideal position that is simply out of my reach.

As I go 'round and 'round, facing my imperfections each after the next, I practice accepting them. Some days those imperfections are fairly minor; on others I can't even seem to blink properly; but short of dislocating a bone, tearing a sinew, or cheating, there are no days on which I will ever be perfect. Except to Pink, of course, to whom we are all perfect on all days.

And this is the whole point of practicing yoga! Despite the fashion industry devoted to it and the dramatic photography slapped all over magazines, yoga is not and never has been about perfection. It's not even about being *cool.* In fact, it is very specifically about being *un*cool. It's about walking into your glass walls and pushing against them, about making progress through practice, which, in turn, means moving upward and onward through the practice of failure.

I know that I will never achieve anything close to a state of Zen, and I may never even get to a place where I can lay quietly and breathe without plotting out a six-episode miniseries in my head, but years of yoga practice *have* gotten me to a place where I am comfortable accepting and learning from failure. The ability to mess up with grace, to be wrong and move on – that may not be Zen, but it's pretty bad*asana.*

Samuel Beckett (the playwright, not the Quantum Leap character) once wrote, "Ever tried. Ever failed. No matter. Try again. Fail again. Fail better." Which is the art of yoga – and life – in a nutshell. You try a pose, you fail a little – or maybe a lot; you try again, and fail a little less, and some days you get even worse, but some later days you start to get better, and over time you not only progress physically, but you also develop a *Buddah*ful skill: the mental strength to accept and embrace failure, the flexibility to forgive yourself and change, and the balance to stay focused and breathe through the ride.

THEORETICAL PHYSICS

TIME WEIGHTS FOR ALL MAN

Time is a flat circle. No, wait; Time is an increasingly hyperbolic "news" magazine. Time is an herb to the blind and spelling-impaired?

Time is all of these things, and also none of them, for time – like color and popularity – is merely a product of our own perception.

We know this because more than a century ago a bored 26-year-old patent clerk started daydreaming and ended up having the best year of his – or of anybody's, really – life. It's a good thing there weren't more people inventing things in Bern around 1905.

In the heart of the summer of that magical year of 1905, that bored patent clerk – who was still bored after publishing a paper in March on the photoelectric effect that would become the foundation for quantum physics (and for which he would win a Nobel Prize) and publishing another paper in early May about Brownian motion – started thinking about Galileo and Newton, and how the motion of objects is relative to the motion of an observer. He then asked a question no one else had ever asked: What about light?

That got him daydreaming about speeding trains, and the universe was changed forever. Literally.

Side rant: what is it with men and their fascination with vehicles? Galileo and Newton determined relative motion by thinking about boats (while a man walking on a ship's deck may travel 10 meters in 10 seconds from his own perspective, he travels much farther to a person on shore also watching the ship sail by), and Einstein used trains to show that a beam of light bouncing from floor to ceiling travels one distance to an observer on the train but a longer distance to an observer watching the train from a hill. Boys and cars, man. It's deeply genetic.

By the end of June 1905, Albert Einstein had published his Special Theory of Relativity, which states that if light truly does always move at a constant rate (which experiments had shown but scientists had been reluctant to accept), then time must be just as relative to the observer as distance and motion and acceptable fashion standards*

Suddenly, a clock was nothing more than a series of countable moments; a second merely an agreed-upon unit that only stays consistent so long as we remain still relative to the time piece.

---

*Shoulder pads, anyone?

As soon as we accelerate that clock out the window, those seconds get longer. So...time flies less as it flies.

Our bodies already know this; the heart is a clock, beating out a series of countable events, and the faster we move the slower time progresses. Stay active, stay young.

Before 1905 played out, Einstein managed to blow minds open a fourth time by proving that mass and energy are on the same spectrum (or, as it is more commonly known, that energy (E) equals mass (m) times the speed of light (c) squared). This equation gave us the power (nuclear power), and Einstein the ability to reach his most influential deduction of all – which, given his work thus far, is certainly saying something.

If light is energy, he thought (paper one), and energy has mass (paper four), then light has mass and should be affected by gravity (which it proved to be – eventually; in 1919, a solar eclipse allowed experimenters to prove that light does indeed bend its path when traveling past a large body such as the sun). And if the path of light is bent by gravity, Einstein continued, then so must time be affected (paper three).

It took a decade to work out the math, but by November 1915 Albert Einstein was able to present his General Theory of Relativity, which tied the fourth dimension (time) to the three we already knew so well (space) and introduced the idea of Space-Time as the fabric of our universe. A fabric that, like a fabric should, gives and curves around heavier objects. The larger a mass, the more it tells both space and time to "get bent." That's gravity.

So if time, like light and space and anything else with mass, is affected by gravity, it makes sense that time itself has mass. Finally! That explains the Sunday evening doldrums, when the weight of the weekend that hangs behind us requires a Herculean effort of will to drag ourselves into Monday morning.

It also explains why, as I try to fall asleep some nights, I can physically feel those ounces of time passing through me – from future, to present, to past – adding their weight to the ever-increasing mass of time that lies behind. One. Heartbeat. At. A. Time. How much farther must I carry that weight toward the unknown destination of my future? Can I keep moving forward as it keeps getting heavier every day? At what point will it weigh too much and drag me to a complete standstill – or backwards?

On these nights, I find it comforting to remember the formula $E = mc^2$, and the fact that the accumulating mass of the past also increases its potential energy. The longer it takes us to get…wherever, the brighter we can burn when we do.

Other times, I just roll over and find a fuzzy cat ass in my face. A cat ass in the face is pretty much the best life has to offer anyway, so really, what's the hurry?

Full-Frontal Nerdity: Extra Credit

FILM (AND AUTHOR) STUDIES

TOTO ECLIPSE OF THE HEART

The Wizard of Oz was my first movie love, and you never forget your first love. But it has also been a major influence throughout my life. According to my mother, I was so terrified of the Wicked Witch of the West as a child that I would hide behind the couch whenever she appeared on screen – but that didn't stop me from still demanding my family watch the film any and every time it aired on TV. My love for the rest was just too strong to let a silly thing like fear keep me away. Thus, the first thing *The Wizard of Oz* gave me was my courage.

That new-found bravery came in handy when I learned that the community children's theatre in my town had chosen L. Frank Baum's classic story for their next production. At age nine, the idea of being on stage was mortifying to me, but the opportunity to play Toto was one I simply could not resist. Yes, Toto; he was my dream role. Sure, other characters are more glamorous, but Toto is the real star – he's in the most scenes – and the true hero of the story. Plus, I wouldn't have to say any lines and in the movie he was basically the 4th-highest-paid actor. No contest.

For weeks, I wore out my storybook cassette tape, playing the narration on our living room stereo and acting out the entire story on the rug, from Toto's perspective. I got the part. It was my first taste of success, my first bite of the acting bug, and my first experience with improv and collaborative storytelling. That play is also how I met the woman who to this day is still my best friend in the world (she played a citizen of the Emerald City). Thus, *The Wizard of Oz* led me, in multiple ways, to my heart.

Time and again I have fallen back on Toto and the gang as I have chased down my heart's desire far from my own backyard. After I completed my first screenplay – on a whim, really, just to see if I could – and the thing wound up being read at several major studios and almost getting made, I was faced with a frightening challenge. Suddenly, people in power knew my writing, and wanted to see what else I could do; I needed another screenplay to prove I wasn't a fluke, but I had not thought that far ahead.

So I turned to what I loved. I wrote an adaptation of Dorothy's story as a coming-of-age romantic comedy, with the Scarecrow, Tin Man, and Lion representing archetypes of imperfect partners. (All brains / no chemistry, perfect but gay, and commitment-phobic, if you're curious.) I also started to develop a sitcom about a girl living in an apartment above a bar called The Rainbow. Both were way too weird for anyone to want to make them, but they kept my career going. Thus, *The Wizard of Oz* has helped me engage and exercise my brain.

Recently, I decided to re-read Baum's original book, which I so enjoyed as a child. Now, as an adult writing movies of my own, the adaptation choices of the 1938 screenwriters are of great interest to me. Most people know that the witch's slippers were changed from silver to ruby for the glory of Technicolor, but did you also know that Glinda is an amalgam of two characters in the book – the North and South witches merged into one? Baum's good witch of the North, Gaylette, is described as someone "everyone loved…but her greatest sorrow was that she could find no one to love in return, since all the men were much too stupid and ugly to mate with one so beautiful and wise." These days* that is my favorite line in the story.

Other changes are more significant. In the books, Oz is multi-colored (blue in the East, yellow in the West, red in the South and green in the middle), but Dorothy does not fly "over the rainbow" to get there – the land just sits trapped in a vast desert. There is a lot more danger in Baum's Oz than in the movie, and, in turn, a lot more killing by the Tin Man and Lion to ward off said danger (there are a fairly disturbing number of chopped-off animal heads). Also, in the book Dorothy is stuck in Oz so long that Uncle Henry has enough time to single-handedly rebuild their one-room farm house before she gets back.

That last bit points to my favorite difference between the screenplay and the original story; in the book, Dorothy's adventure is real, while in the film they chose to make it a dream. The

---

*These single days

reason I love this change is because, by doing so, *The Wizard of Oz* (the film) managed to both introduce the single most memorable line in movie history and completely subvert its message at the same time. Dorothy's mantra is "There's no place like home," but by populating Kansas with the same actors who portray the denizens of Oz, the film ends up making the very real statement that everywhere – even over the rainbow – is in fact *just like home*. It becomes a cinematic manifestation of the old proverb, "No matter where you go, there you are." Location is irrelevant; the only real change happens within.

Think you need intelligence, or compassion, or nerve? All you really need is to recognize those things in yourself. What is Dorothy's lesson before she can click her heels? That she need not search for her heart's desire anywhere but where she is; if the answer isn't within her already, it isn't anywhere. Dorothy, the Scarecrow, the Tin Man, and the Lion all learn that your problems are your problems wherever you go, and the solutions have been inside of you all along. *Where* you are is irrelevant, because *who* you are is what matters.

Los Angeles is a very difficult place to live – doubly so if you have a soul – and the film industry is downright hostile. Between dating and working here since college, I have had the urge to run away roughly once every week for more than a dozen years. *The Wizard of Oz* has stopped me every time, because I know getting out of here won't really change anything that matters. Los Angeles isn't my home, but neither is any physical place.

What L. Frank Baum meant when he wrote "there is no place like home" is that nothing else in the world compares to the feeling that you belong somewhere. In that sense, home is an energy, not a place. It is family, yes, but not just traditional family (Dorothy is an adopted orphan, after all). Home is the people who love us, and the people we love in return – with any luck, including ourselves. I never feel more myself than when I am experiencing this story, revisiting all of the memories and the people I associate with our history. Thus, *The Wizard of Oz* brings me home.

Thanks, Toto.

ABOUT THE AUTHOR:

K.S. Wiswell went into Harvard to become a cryptographer and came out with a BA in English. Along the way she studied physics, linguistics, philosophy, mythology, and marching band. After three years in the corporate world, she escaped to Los Angeles and joined the Second City, because improv is cheaper than therapy. She remains an over-educated comedy writer who teaches logic to balance the insanity. Over the years, she has been told by serious men that she is "pretty smart for a girl," "pretty funny for a girl," and once (after a disastrous Mary Lou Retton-inspired haircut) "pretty cute for a boy." All of which is pretty dumb for a society, so she has made it her mission to promote through her writing the reality that Smart is indeed Sexy.

She lives, writes, and teaches in Los Angeles, accompanied by a car named Frodo and her two rescue cats, Martini and Olive.

ACKNOWLEDGMENTS:

This book would not have been possible without the incredible lifetime of support I've received from my parents. Thanks for not only resisting the urge to ask me when I'm going to go back to a real job, but for being the ones who encouraged me to quit the corporate world in the first place and instead chase my dreams. You're the best bad influences a kid could ever hope for.

Thanks to Ellenor, for being my Samwise Gamgee, and to my readers Molly and Kyle for giving me their time, thoughts, friendship, and daily support out here in the land of la la. And all my love and gratitude to my nephews (as well as their parents) for giving me constant inspiration to create something worthwhile for the future generations.

I'm grateful to all my students, who teach me to keep questioning myself every single day, and to my college band-mate Shalla, for suggesting I go after that first teaching job and thus inadvertently starting me down the path that ultimately led to the creation and publication of this book. While I'm at it, my thanks to the Harvard Band as a whole, for keeping me sane and laughing through college, and ingraining the concept of "shorter and funnier" into my very soul. *Illegitimum non carborundum,* forever.

Finally, my thanks to Maureen, Amy, and the whole fabulous team at 750 Publishing, for first saying yes to my wacky proposal, and then embracing the idea every step of the way. Just when you think you've got things all figured out, people go and surprise you with opportunities you never could have imagined. How lucky we are to be a part of it all; thank you.

Made in the USA
San Bernardino, CA
10 November 2019